COOKING WITH CRAFT BEER

Stevan Paul
Torsten Goffin
Daniela Haug

RECIPES
Stevan Paul

TEXT
Torsten Goffin

PHOTOGRAPHY
Daniela Haug

COOKING WITH CRAFT BEER

HORS D'OEUVRES & APPETISERS

FISH & SEAFOOD

MEAT & ROTISSERIE

CLASSIC BEER SNACKS

SWEETS & DESSERTS

Wurst&Bier
Markthalle Neun

PALE ALE

'HE WHO DRINKS BEER, LIVES TO ONE HUNDRED'

ITALIAN SAYING

Without question – rarely has there been so much beer around as there is now! Hardly a weekend passes by without somewhere around the world thousands of people gathering to try beer together at festivals, hardly a month without a brewery somewhere launching the production of unique handcrafted beers far removed from the uniformity of most of the beer we see advertised on the television.

Craft beer is the name given to this phenomenon, whose roots lie on the other side of the Atlantic from Europe. It all began there more than 30 years ago, as a defiant reaction against the extreme monotony of the American beer landscape. Meanwhile, as the worldwide craft beer movement grew up in other parts of the world, including in the UK and Australia, in the land of its origins, this movement became the everyday beer culture – there's hardly a supermarket in the United States these days that doesn't offer shelves filled with a comprehensive selection of craft beers from all over the country.

Here in Germany we're still a long way removed from that. But also in Europe you'll more often find India pale ale (IPA), porter, gose, lambic, stout and ale: beers produced with great dedication and passion – brewed by people who see beer first and foremost as a valuable cultural possession and not as a purely profit-making product.

In this book we want to introduce some of the protagonists in this movement from around the world – a colourful mix of leaders and newcomers, along with long-established traditional breweries.

We also of course have a look at their products: the beer. Above all we do this by considering an aspect that until now has often been given short shrift when talking about craft beer: the food that matches it.

And so this book contains – along with some useful facts about beer and brewing styles – recipes from Stevan Paul specially developed for cooking with beer, with clear suggestions for which beer can be combined with which dishes. One particularly important point though: however clear the individual suggestions might be, we couldn't be further from being dogmatic. We don't want to give you any absolutely definitive rules, but rather provide ideas. Above all, however, we want to inspire you to discover, through your own culinary expeditions, the exciting world and colourful variety of the newly awakened brewing culture.

BREWERIES

Feral Brewing
Private Landbrauerei Schönram
The Kernel Brewery
Landbrauhaus Hofstetten
Bogk-Bier Private Brewery
BRLO
Brasserie Cantillon
Schneider Weisse
Ale-Mania
Kehrwieder Kreativbrauerei
Vormann
Uerige
Brouwerij de Molen
Sierra Nevada

0
20
40
60
80
100
120
SCHULZ
C
157643

THE POT ON THE FIRE

THE ORIGINS OF BREWING

'In prehistoric times people gathered in the evenings around the fire with a pot of porridge. If they pushed it a little closer to the fire, they got bread, if they pushed it a little further away, they got beer.'

This is how Berliner weisse brewer Andreas Bogk describes the beginning of beer culture. Admittedly, his description is very shortened here – it nevertheless makes two points crystal clear: on the one hand the close relationship between brewing and baking, and on the other the extremely long period in which humankind has busied itself with brewing. The oldest records on the subject are about 6000 years old and come from the Sumerians – anthropologists and archaeologists assume, however, that the history of brewing (and that of baking) had already begun with the change of lifestyle from hunter-gatherer to growing crops and raising animals – we humans have thus been concocting beer for at least 11,000 years. A pot is left standing with cooked cereals – and a few days later the porridge is discovered bubbling away dangerously, to bafflingly exhilarating effect. This is presumably the moment of birth for all beers.

But how exactly did that happen? And is brewing beer actually that easy? In principle, yes is the answer. In practice, however, it reads more like the relationship status of many a Facebook member: *It's complicated!* In any case, the basis of each beer creation is alcoholic fermentation – that is the conversion of glucose into carbon dioxide and ethanol by yeasts. The yeasts necessary for this process are everywhere in the air. For this reason, liquids that contain glucose automatically begin to ferment after a short time. This is called spontaneous fermentation, and some beers, for example Belgian lambic, are still fermented this way today. But in that case, why doesn't any piece of yeast dough left to rise for longer not become an alcohol-filled mixture within a short time?

Very simply, because yeast can only ferment glucose – and there's hardly any available in cereals. Because to shield the energy-rich glucose in cereal grains from yeasts and other 'robbers', evolution developed a special form of glucose storage: starch. It's actually nothing more than long chains of glucose molecules, but nevertheless protected in that way from yeasts. The starches will only become single glucose molecules again at precisely the moment the energy stored in them is needed – by the germinating shoot. This occurs with the help of certain enzymes that are already present in the seed in trace amounts, but they'll be produced in full quantity only when needed. Whoever wants to brew beer must therefore ensure that the starches in the grain can be converted to glucose.

And that's exactly what occurs during malting, the first important step on the way to beer. It's importance is indicated by the fact that the official title of the brewer's trade in Germany is 'brewer and malter'. But although this description binds the two jobs inextricably together, malting has become the task of specialists, and very few breweries still do their own malting. Among the rare exceptions is the Augustiner-Bräu brewery in Munich, which still employs the traditional *Tennenmalz* procedure which, although considered very aromatic, on the grounds of efficiency and cost, is rarely still used.

The basic principle of malting is simple: through the supply of moisture and a constant temperature the grains begin to shoot, so that the seed begins to produce the enzymes necessary for the breakdown of starch. The shooting is then stopped by kiln-drying, before the seeds themselves can convert the starches they contain. In earlier times the moist malt was dried over an open fire – and a strong flavour of smoke in the end product was the unavoidable consequence. Such smoked malts are still part of certain beer recipes today. In Bamberg there have even been beers brewed exclusively with smoked malt. But the temperature during drying has a strong influence on the aromatic characteristics and the colour of the malt. Every pot-roast lover and baker of bread knows the Maillard reaction, in which carbohydrate and protein caramelise and good-tasting toasty substances develop when a certain temperature is reached. With what's called black (or roasted) malt, this is precisely what happens.

The two first steps in authentic brewing are milling and mashing. The rough grinding of the chosen malt mixture – for a good beer, different types of malt bringing different styles and characteristics are usually added to the composition – brings starches and enzymes together. The slow heating releases the component glucose molecules and simultaneously activates different enzymes at certain temperature levels. With periods called rests – where certain temperature levels are maintained – the brewer gives the enzymes the opportunity to have an effect and thus controls factors in the final beer, such as foam development and storage time, but also clarity and sweetness. Mashing ends with heating to about 75°C (167°F), which deactivates all the available enzymes in the liquid, and then with lautering, the separation of the hard remains of the grains from the liquid. We're left with the residual grain, which is often used as cattle feed, and what we call the first wort – the liquid in which the malt sugars are now found, which will later be fermented by yeasts to make alcohol.

Before that though, the wort will be mixed with hops and boiled. On the one hand this releases the desired bitter substances from the hops that will flavour the beer and lend it stability, while on the other it kills any shoots brought inadvertently with the malt and destroys for good any remaining active enzymes. During the boiling process and the consequent reduction in liquid, the brewer can also control the sugar content of the boiled wort – and thus the alcohol content of the final beer.

In the settling stage the liquid is again separated from the solids, such as the hops. The beer is then cooled. Earlier this happened in vessels called coolships – large copper basins usually right under the roof of the brewery – but today cooling usually occurs in tanks. A further addition of hops to enhance the flavour of the beer often occurs here. Then it's finally time for the actual fermentation. This starts either through spontaneous inoculation with yeasts from the surrounding environment, or, more usually, through the addition of specific yeast strains. The brewer will control the temperature to suit the composition of the yeast.

Until the end of the nineteenth century, the brewing style customary in most regions was top-fermenting, in which yeasts are used that need a room temperature of 15–20°C (59–68°F) to work optimally. They are called top-fermenting because during the course of fermentation they float on the surface of the liquid. In Bavaria, with its cold winters and the possibility of ice forming on a top-fermenting yeast during long periods in a cave cellar, they instead used the bottom-fermenting style, which requires a fermentation temperature of 4–9°C (39–48°F). In this case the yeasts settle to the bottom of the fermenting vat near the end. Bottom-fermented beers take longer to reach maturity, which is why in English the generic term for them is 'lager', the German for storeroom. In comparison with their top-fermented colleagues, they keep for longer – which apart from the clear and fresh flavour is certainly one reason for their increased dominance. This was made possible by the invention at the end of the nineteenth century of mechanical cooling, making cold conditions available whatever the season or region.

These days the majority of beer based on barley malt is bottom-fermented, and only wheat beers and some regional specialties, such as altbier, kölsch or British ales, have retained top-fermenting processes. But whether top- or bottom-fermented, the yeasts transformed by fermentation – or more precisely the by-products of fermentation – are, beside the flavours of malt and hops, the third big factor in the taste profile of finished beers.

To reach this stage of completion, the green or young beer, as it's called after the main fermentation stage, is left to mature for a certain time at cool temperatures in vessels called bright beer tanks. Small amounts of remaining glucose will be fermented by the yeasts during this secondary fermentation, and the carbon dioxide produced saturates the beer. Particularly with craft beer, a last addition of hops is made at this stage. With the process called dry or cold hopping, the fleeting, fruity, ethereal aroma of the hops, which during the boiling stage is otherwise lost, is reintroduced. Beers with an unusually intense fruity flavour are the result.

At the end of this lagering phase the beer is finally ready to be transferred to bottles or casks. Depending on the style of beer, this will be first purified – that is, filtered completely clear – or even left with a certain amount of yeast in the beer. The latter is always true for beers that undergo bottle fermentation, for example, because they are fermented in open vessels rather than under pressure in wooden casks, and so must still – like Champagne – produce carbon dioxide in the bottle in order to develop the desired effervescence. A reseeding in the form of wort or glucose gives the yeast the necessary supplementary nourishment.

There is no question: on its long way through the millennia – from the first accidentally fermented stone-age pot of porridge all the way to the beer we know today – a lot has happened. But in principle, all that's needed to brew beer today is still nothing more than a large pot and the possibility of heating it slowly and in a controlled way. As thousands of hobby brewers worldwide prove again and again, every day.

THE BREWER'S 'GREEN GOLD'

HOW HOPS MADE THEIR WAY INTO BEER

'... as a result of its own bitterness it keeps some putrefactions from drinks, to which it may be added, so that they may last so much longer.'

HILDEGARD VON BINGEN

And so Hildegard von Bingen already knew about the microbiologically stabilising effect of hops – and yet the polymaths resisted the addition of hops to beer. They instead recommended ash-tree leaves and other herbs as stabilisers and seasonings for beer, which at that time was mostly brewed using oats.

However inseparable the marriage between hops and malt might now seem, at the beginning of brewing's history they were not even a couple. Instead, in Germany beer was usually brewed with fruit, and an often fierce mixture of herbs that didn't go together well and which sometimes contained psychotropic substances, such as stinking nightshade.

Only when, in the middle of the thirteenth century, the Bremen Hanseatic League began to export beer with hops through the then world trade centre of Bruges, did the triumphal march of hops start – finally marking, together with the change from oats to barley, the beginning of beer as we know it. The end point of this development was the Bavarian *Reinheitsgebot* (Purity Law) of 1516, that only allowed, besides water, hops and barley as basic ingredients for brewing beer.

Today worldwide, almost 50,000 hectares (123,000 acres) are devoted to about 90,000 tonnes of hop plants, which can grow to 8 metres (26 feet). They are harvested at 1 metre (39 inches) high. More than a third of these are produced in Germany. It follows that here you'll also find the largest area devoted to growing hops in the world, in the Hallertau region, south of the Danube between Ingolstadt and Regensburg. It is an agricultural landscape of around 2400 square kilometres (926 square miles), whose common concern since the eighth century has been growing hops. Hops and beer have left their traces on the Hallertau in many ways, in the form of the world's oldest monastic brewery in Weltenburg, for example, or in the form of the German Hop Museum in Wolnzach (for more see www.hopfenland-hallertau.de). But above all, of course, in the form of about 15,000 hectares (37,000 acres) of hopfields, which offer an imposing sight worth seeing, especially just before the harvest between the end of August and the end of September.

There are more than 200 different varieties of hop, among which two main groups are recognised: those called bitter hops, with a high as possible content of alpha acid (the substance that provides the majority of the bitterness and conservative effect); and those called aromatic hops, which contain less alpha acid and appreciably more essential oils and other aromatic substances. The second group is inextricably bound to the craft beer revolution.

But more about that in the next chapter...

IN THE BEGINNING WAS AN IPA

'For lots of people their first contact with craft beer is like discovering a whole new type of music they've never heard before, but one that will accompany them for the rest of their life. I mean, what could be more beautiful?'

GARRETT OLIVER, BROOKLYN BREWERY

If you talk to craft-beer lovers or even craft-beer brewers, a surprising number of them will remember exactly their lightbulb moment – the beer that forever changed their view of the world of brewing. For Australian Brendan Varis of Feral Brewing it was, for example, the 'delirium tremens', of a Belgian classic: 'After I'd drunk it, I spent a whole week's wages just to try other beers I'd never tasted before until then!'

With many beer fans, when the conversation turns to what started their love and passion for handcrafted beer, you hear the same three letters surprisingly often: IPA. They stand for India pale ale – the beer style that more than any other represents the phenomenon of craft beer. This is no accident, for the hop-dominated IPAs demonstrate even before the first taste their powerful qualitative lead over anything else sold under the beer label. The enormously varied and complex bouquet of a typical IPA announces a taste sensation that most beer drinkers have until that moment never experienced. Grass-green herbal notes, citrus or exotic mango or passionfruit – IPAs offer an aromatic complexity that you otherwise find only in the best wines. An almost disturbingly luxurious variety of aromas extends over the palate. There the fruit aromas are joined by an unexpectedly intense bitterness – which in time will be systematically driven out by successive bursts of radicchio, endive (chicory) and asparagus, and which especially for the novice can take some getting used to.

In the emergence of this imposing beer style there are legends. It originated during British colonial rule in India, so the story goes. The slightly increased alcohol content and the above-average strength of the hopping were originally measures to keep the beer microbiologically stable on the long voyage from England to India. It was, so to speak, a concentrated beer, brewed with the intention of thinning it down to normal strength at the destination. But the strong-tasting beer found great favour in its undiluted form – and thus IPA was born. However beautiful and comprehensively specific the points of this story might sound, it hasn't been verified historically. What is clear, however, is that the practice of cold hopping after the conclusion of the brewing process is closely linked to the original IPAs and most certainly also served to improve storage on sea voyages.

In connection with new, high-aromatic hop cultivars such as Cascade, this technique was rediscovered in the United States at the beginning of the 1980s. The Anchor Brewing Company in San Francisco produced its Christmas Ale in 1975; and in 1980 Sierra Nevada brought its Pale Ale to the market, which in the meantime has become widely available in other parts of the world. Only a year later came Celebration, the first IPA. The use of this new hopping technique, which is marked by a relatively low content of alpha acid (the substance that makes the beer bitter) and a high proportion of aromatic essential oils, is without doubt one of the central pillars upon which the craft beer revolution rests to this day.

That it has its beginnings in of all places the United States is in a nutshell thanks to a deficiency – however paradoxical that might sound. Because when in 1979, under President Jimmy Carter, homebrewing was again legalised in the United States (Alabama and Mississippi still maintained the ban, which dated from the days of Prohibition in the 1920s, until 2013), there were in the whole of the USA only 90 breweries left. And most of the remaining mass-produced products were free of depth, quality or even soul. At the same time, reasonable prices for flights meant that more and more Americans were made aware of Europe and its diverse beer culture. The knowledge that something was missing was thus awoken. The consequence: self-help brewing and the foundation of a multitude of new breweries. By the mid-1990s, the number had grown again to more than 500; today there are more than 3500.

For a long time only Pale Ale and IPA were brewed. Apart from top-fermented stout and porter, which also have their origins in the Anglo-Saxon tradition, the Americans helped themselves freely to any convention that seemed worthwhile: Belgian beer styles such as abbey beer or witbier as well as German styles such as helles or kölsch. The latest big trend there is sour beer. One result of the craft-beer boom there was impossible to predict: craft beer now makes up around 11 per cent of the volume of all beer brewed in the United States and proudly generates 22 per cent of the industry's turnover.

It's not without a certain irony that of all places the United States, the supposed stronghold of beer *un*culture, has become the guardian and renewer of brewing traditions. Inspired by the events there, the trend eventually reached the other side of the Atlantic. Although for the time being we can only dream of numbers like those in the United States, in Europe, too, small and microbrewery start-ups are springing up like mushrooms. And finally the local craft-beer scene is no longer modelling itself narrowly on the American example. In Germany brewers have set themselves on the path of rediscovering old methods, to preserve them or – inspired by the undogmatic American love of experimentation – to interpret them in a modern way through creative experimentation. This takes many in the scene a long way from the progress-hindering corset of the Purity Law.

BITTER-SWEET SYMPHONY

'Well-hopped beers cut like a knife through heavy sauces, fats and oils. They leave behind a cleansed and refreshed palate rather than numbing it.'

GARRETT OLIVER, BROOKLYN BREWERY

In 2010 a beer did the rounds that for the first time drew particular attention among gourmet circles. It was called Inedit, it came from the Spanish brewing company Estrella Damm and was brewed in the style of a Belgian witbier. The reason for the great interest: the brewing recipe was developed in association with Ferran Adrià, the greatest culinary innovator of the last three decades. In fact, it was a beer that, according to its self-promotion, was suitable to accompany dishes from the gourmet kitchen. Whether you can meet this high claim in general terms with a single beer may rightfully be doubted. Inedit was the only beer to have trodden the gourmet stage.

Since then a lot has happened. The Danish craft-beer pioneer Mikkeller, together with a top Copenhagen restaurant, brought out a *MAD*-magazine series of five beers devoted to the five tastes (sour, sweet, salty, bitter and umami); and more recently, in collaboration with the Belgian brewery Lindemans, released Spontanbasil, a gueuze-style beer fermented with basil that forces itself into food pairings like no other beer. The top chefs worldwide are discovering this theme as a welcome addition to their restaurants. 'I don't think beer will ever replace wine,' says René Redzepi, chef of Noma in Copenhagen, the restaurant named best in the world numerous times, 'but I believe that in the future it will be much more clearly present.'

And how does the food pairing work? Let's begin with the most important rule: there are no rules. At least none that are universally valid. Whichever combination both tastes good to and pleases a certain individual is, in that moment, the right one for that person. And this is how the notes on beer styles and particular recommendations in the following recipes should be interpreted: as encouragement and stimulus for your own journeys and experiments.

But there are a few basic principles that are helpful in the successful combination of dishes with beer: a happy *balance* is the basis of a good food pairing. It seems a truism – and yet it's important to repeat it – that each drink and dish should weigh in with the same intensity of taste. A heavy imperial stout, for example, will kill the delicate flavours of a freshwater fish terrine, just as a ripe munster cheese will destroy the lightness of a subtly hopped wheat beer.

An interesting *contrast*, however, can make a beer–dish combination extremely exciting. When, for example, the fresh sourness of a wheat beer meets the clear sweetness of caramelised onion. Or the refreshingly dry bitterness of a classic altbier meets the fatty heaviness of roast pork. Or when the exotic fruitiness of an IPA is married with the strong spiciness of a Thai curry. A certain *tension* between plate and glass is indispensable for the combination of two different elements to blend on the palate into something bigger.

The last element in successful food pairing makes the most of the play between aromatic *parallels*. Many of the recommendations in the recipe section of this book work on this principle. Fruit flavours from aromatic hops – mango, mandarin and citrus, for example – that find their equivalent on the plate; smoky notes from fish or meat that are reflected in the smoked-malt parts of a beer; chocolate or coffee notes in a stout that build a bridge to a dessert. It's always important in such cases that on the one hand the analogy makes a flavour connection but on the other that each element retains sufficient individuality to avoid a mere doubling – and thus dull food.

An exception is cooking *with* beer. Because in contrast to wine, which is frequently used in cooking sauces or soups and as a marinade, many, if not all, beers distinguish themselves through a particular bitterness. In food pairing this is highly desirable as a counterpoint, for example to fat, although in the saucepan and on the plate they can interfere with one another, especially when they are even more concentrated through reduction in sauces. The same goes, if not to such a great degree, for the residual sweetness or toasty notes in some beers.

As a rule of thumb, let's say this: everywhere you would make a reduction with wine – that is, rapid evaporation of the liquid from the saucepan – you should take care if using a strongly hopped beer instead. To coin a phrase: the stronger the reduction, the lighter the hopping of the beer. When, on the other hand, beer will be substituted in only small amounts – comparable to a shot of cognac or whisky in a pepper cream sauce – the marked hop bitterness of an IPA, for example, can lend a very interesting depth of flavour.

A second, more important difference from wine is that many beers lack the refreshing sourness so freely available with wine. A simple swap of beer for wine is therefore not advisable for most recipes. But there is one group of beers with which this problem doesn't arise. They are the – *nomen est omen* – sour beers. It is thus anything but an accident that Jean-Pierre van Roy, owner of the Brussels sour beer specialist Cantillon, says that no other beers go with cooking like lambic and gueuze. Not only does their sourness makes them suitable for use in the cooking pot, but also their lack of bitterness, thanks to long maturation in barrels.

In conclusion, we repeat: our aim isn't to set up definite rules. With this book we want above all to do one thing: inspire you to trust your own tastes and set out on a tour of discovery of the extremely varied world of beer.

28
HOG

IPA GLASS

Perfect for IPAs, ales and cold-hopped lagers.

BEER TULIP

For pilsners, and for all others a good compromise.

STOUT GLASS

For rust-coloured styles such as stout, porter and dark bock.

AMERICAN WHEAT-BEER GLASS

For aromatic wheat beers, but also goses/sour beers.

LAGER GLASS

For pale and amber-coloured lagers.

BALLOON GLASS

For fruit-coloured wine hybrids.

ALTBIER GLASS

Obligatory in Düsseldorf for altbier and sticke alt.

BOTTLE

Only for huge thirsts and other emergencies.

WHEAT-BEER GLASS

For kristallweizen (crystal white) and hefeweizen (cloudy white) beers. Clinked at the bottom.

PINT

For British beers. The word for both the glass shape and the amount.

KÖLSCH POLE

Obligatory for kölsch. Also mocked as a 'test tube'.

TEKU POKAL

Widespread universal glass for tastings.

BEER CULTURE AND GLASS CULTURE

'It's amazing how a polished rim on a glass affects the enjoyment of a beer. The taste becomes more aromatic, the texture creamier. It spells the end of the rolled rim we know from conventional glasses.'

SYLVIA KOPP, BERLIN BEER ACADEMY

It's not easy to make Sylvia Kopp, beer sommelier and the Brewers Association's newly named ambassador for American craft beer, this euphoric. But on the day of a tasting with different beer glasses at Heidenpeters in the Berlin Market Hall Nine she made no secret of how struck she was by the stark contrast between conventional glasses and those developed for different beer styles.

She was invited there by Spiegelau, a glass producer that has, in collaboration with leading American craft-beer brewers – including greats like Ken Grossman of Sierra Nevada – developed glasses especially for different craft-beer styles. The idea had spread through the beer world that to wine lovers had seemed self-evident for a long time – that there cannot be an optimal glass perfectly suited to each different wine style. Similarly different beer styles place different demands on the glass shape, at least when you want to get the most enjoyment possible from a beer.

Out of a long series of tests, in which more than 150 different shapes were tried and the unsuitable ones repeatedly rejected, three different glass shapes for different craft-beer styles finally crystallised. One optimised for the enjoyment of IPAs or ales, one for stouts and porters, and one for the aromatic wheat beers, such as Belgian witbiers. Common to all of these glasses is the pleasing thinness of the walls, reminiscent of good wine glasses. Also known from better wine glasses is the polished rim, which marks all the craft-beer glasses in this Beer Classics series (as does their rather classical shapes). Only someone who has tried the same beer from a glass with and without a rolled rim can understand how much this rim affects enjoyment of the beer.

Obviously you can also enjoy craft beer without specially shelling out for the three different glasses. To get started, though, you can make use of two of the most important insights offered by these special craft-beer glasses: it's worth avoiding a bulging rolled rim and walls that are too thick. For this reason, those who make use of wine glasses, which they perhaps already have to hand, for craft beer, are often surprised how much more enjoyable some beers are in comparison to drinking them out of standard beer glasses – even when wine glasses used in this way don't reach the heights of the craft-beer glasses that have been optimised in their size and basic shape.

One thing you should never do with exquisite specialty craft beers: drink them direct out of the bottle or even can. Because that doesn't allow the varied and complex aromas that mark every good craft beer the chance to reveal themselves.

PALE ALE

BeerBods
WIPER AND TRUE

INDIA PALE ALE

INVITATION TO A TASTING

'Observation is the basis of knowledge.'

JOHANN HEINRICH PESTALOZZI

After so much about the theory, history and nature of craft beers, it's time to put them into practice. But no number of words about the merits of craft beers can replace the impression of your own taste test.

What for a long time was the biggest hindrance to the spread of craft beers – availability – has in recent times clearly improved. Hardly a week goes by without a new craft-beer specialist shop opening somewhere, and there is hardly a bottleshop now without at least a small corner dedicated to craft beers. Also the number of distributors has increased. In addition, many internet stores offer beginner packages, and it would be wonderful if virtual tasting communities like the British BeerBods (www.beerbods.co.uk) were soon established in other countries too. On a subscription basis, BeerBod members – each by themselves and yet all virtually together – taste exciting beers each week and have an intense online exchange about them.

In the same way, for the most instructive tasting experience it's worth trying several beers – whether from your local specialist shop or from the internet – at the same time. Because nothing assists the perception of differences – and with that the acquisition of knowledge – as much as the possibility of a direct comparison.

The principle of direct comparison with the aim of learning more can bring great joy in many ways. It's tremendously exciting to try a so-called TV pilsner (that is, one from a big brand advertised widely on TV) right beside a top pilsner such as that from the Private Landbrauerei Schönram. Even perhaps a blind test, without knowing which beer is in which glass, as it's done in professional wine tastings. Or you could compare American IPAs with their German counterparts. Or from the same brewery the pale ales with their stronger siblings the IPAs. The possibilities for deepening your knowledge are enormous.

If, instead, you're firstly looking for a rough orientation in the wider field of craft beer, we recommend trying the three Spiegelau glasses mentioned in the previous chapter. If in the one test you taste, one after the other: an IPA, for example Torpedo Extra by Sierra Nevada or Punk IPA by BrewDog; a stout such as that from BRLO or Schönramer; and a witbier like the Belgian Blanche de Namur or Hoegaarden, with only three different beers you will have uncovered a truly wide spectrum of the craft-beer world.

Independent of which type of tasting you choose, a pure comparison at home on your own can still work, although it won't bring true joy. For a successful tasting you need friends, because they not only increase the number of beers you can taste but also increase the number of impressions and opinions. Tasting in a group forces you to think through the diverse taste impressions so that you can also *describe* them – and that ensures that you remember them permanently. Above all, though, because enthusiasm shared is enthusiasm doubled, at least.

RECIPES

ASPARAGUS SALAD WITH SMOKED HAM ON TOASTED BUTTER BRIOCHE*

INGREDIENTS
Serves 2–4

500 g (1 lb 2 oz) fresh regional white asparagus
1 French shallot
2 tablespoons oil
pinch of salt
about 1 tablespoon white wine vinegar
1 tablespoon helles (bright) beer
1 teaspoon sugar
3 tablespoons olive oil, plus extra for drizzling
1–2 chervil sprigs
4 slices brioche loaf
4 rashers (slices) smoked ham

*

Brioche
(from the French broyer = to knead) has existed in France since at least the fifteenth century. The normally round, butter-soft yeast-baked items have in the meantime also become available from well-stocked bakeries in loaves – very similar to toasting bread, but in its buttery taste and fluffy texture far superior! If you can't get brioche, you can try this recipe with ordinary sliced bread.

A toast to German–French friendship! With toasted brioche, white asparagus and smoked ham.

PREPARATION
25 minutes

METHOD

Peel the asparagus with a vegetable peeler, and cut off any dried-out ends. Cut the asparagus on an angle into quite thick pieces. Peel and finely dice the shallots.

Heat the oil in a frying pan, then add the shallots, asparagus and salt. Stir over medium heat for 3–4 minutes. The asparagus should still have a little bite. Set aside.

Make a vinaigrette by stirring together the vinegar, beer, sugar and olive oil, then mix with the still-warm asparagus. Finely chop the chervil leaves and mix them in. Taste and season with salt and more vinegar if necessary.

Toast the brioche in a toaster, drizzle with a little extra olive oil and top with the salad. Add the ham slices on top and serve.

BEER STYLES: Pale ale, IPA, helles, pilsner.

SPECIAL RECOMMENDATION: Brew by Numbers 11/03 Session IPA – Mosaic, London, UK. Lots of hop aroma but not too much alcohol to accompany perfectly cooked asparagus and smoked ham.

Asparagus salad with smoked ham on toasted butter brioche

Fried little fish on cream cheese bread

FRIED LITTLE FISH ON CREAM CHEESE BREAD

Depending on what you can get at your local market, in this recipe you can pan-fry small anchovies, sardines or smelt until crisp and lay them on wholemeal (whole-wheat) bread with cream cheese and a sultana (golden raisin) vinaigrette. The combination of crisp, creamy and sweet–sour with tangy malty bread tastes particularly good when served with a cold crisp beer.

INGREDIENTS

Makes 4–6 slices

- 50 g (1¾ oz) sultanas (golden raisins)
- 150 ml (5 fl oz) beer, plus 2 tablespoons extra
- 2 tablespoons honey
- 1 tablespoon beer vinegar, white wine vinegar or fruit vinegar
- 1 tablespoon sharp mustard
- 60 ml (2 fl oz/¼ cup) olive oil
- salt
- 4–6 slices wholemeal (whole-wheat) bread
- 80–100 g (2¾–3½ oz) cream cheese
- 500 g (1 lb 2 oz) cleaned and gutted small anchovies, smelt or sardines
- 80 g (2¾ oz) rye flour
- 40 g (1½ oz) butter
- 90 ml (3 fl oz) sunflower oil
- freshly ground black pepper

PREPARATION

25 minutes

METHOD

Wash the sultanas in hot water. Add them to the beer and half the honey in a saucepan, and boil until the liquid evaporates. Make a vinaigrette by stirring together the extra beer, remaining honey, beer vinegar, mustard and olive oil, then add salt to taste. Add the hot sultanas then set aside.

Spread the bread with the cream cheese.

Preheat the oven to 80 °C (180 °F). Rinse the fish thoroughly in cold water then toss in the rye flour while still wet. Heat the butter and sunflower oil in a large frying pan over medium heat and fry the fish in batches for 4–6 minutes until golden brown. Drain on paper towel and sprinkle with salt. Keep the fried fish in the warm oven while cooking the next batch.

Lay the fish on the bread, drizzle with the vinaigrette and season with pepper to taste. Serve immediately.

BEER STYLES: Sour beers, but also paler beers with hop notes, gose, pilsner, kölsch, lager.

SPECIAL RECOMMENDATION: Liefmans' Goudenband from Belgium, with a subtle sourness on the one hand and strong malt and fruit aromas on the other, mirrors the character of this dish perfectly. Those who prefer it a bit lighter, choose the salty/sour gose from Westbrook Brewing, South Carolina, USA.

Coppa crispbreads with pear slices and olive oil

COPPA CRISPBREADS WITH PEAR SLICES AND OLIVE OIL

Extremely delicate aromatic coppa jostles with fresh pear slices on toasted flatbread strips, flavoured with your best olive oil. These are an elegant snack for a lovely evening on the balcony.*

PREPARATION
15 minutes

METHOD
Make a vinaigrette by stirring together the pear juice, mustard, vinegar, honey and olive oil. Cut the unpeeled pear into thin slices, discarding the core. Add the pear pieces to the vinaigrette.

Cut the flatbread lengthways into 1 cm (½ in) wide strips and drizzle with some extra olive oil. Toast under the grill (broiler) until golden brown – they toast quickly, so watch carefully. Top the toast with the coppa and the pear slices. Drizzle over the extra olive oil, season with pepper to taste and serve.

BEER STYLES: Strong, yeast-flavoured beers such as Belgian Saison, Dubbel or Tripel, but also bottle-fermented wheat beers with their higher alcohol content.

SPECIAL RECOMMENDATION: Gumballhead by Three Floyds Brewing Company, Indiana, USA – a refreshing, crisp wheat with a decent citrus aroma. Or the unfortunately very rare Amber Weizenbock by specialist brewer Andreas Gänstaller from the southern Franconian region of Germany, a beer with a strong fullness that goes beautifully with the toast and fruit flavours of the bread.

INGREDIENTS
Serves 2–4

3 tablespoons pear juice
1 teaspoon mustard
1 teaspoon fruit vinegar
1 teaspoon honey
1 tablespoon olive oil, plus extra for drizzling
1 green pear
½ flatbread
80–120 g (2¾–4½ oz) coppa, thinly sliced
freshly ground black pepper

*

Coppa
is an Italian ham made from pig shoulder, which is matured and stored in cloths soaked in white wine. Instead of coppa, the toasted bread would also go well with pancetta, bündnerfleisch (air-dried beef) or Tyrolean ham, or any mild air-dried ham.

STRONGLY HOPPED

INDIA PALE ALE

Also called IPA for short, this usually dark-amber archetype of a craft beer is a taste shock at first contact. For many, it's their awakening to the world of craft beer. American aromatic hops determine the taste, which can be rather floral–fruity at times and at others uncompromising in its strong bitterness – but always with an impressive intensity.

ORIGIN	England
CHARACTER	Floral–fruity to intensely bitter
FERMENTATION	Top-fermented
ALCOHOL CONTENT	5.5–8% Vol.
DRINKING TEMP	8–11°C (46–52°F)
BEST GLASS	IPA glass
EXAMPLES	Sierra Nevada's Torpedo Extra IPA, Riedenburger's Dolden Sud, BrauKunstKeller's Amarsi, Brauprojekt 777's Triple Seven
RECIPES	Cheeseburger (p. 144), Rillettes (p. 182), Smoked Trout (p. 73), Eel (p. 88), Mango with Marzipan Crumbs (p. 237)
VARIANTS	Double, triple or imperial IPA (stronger), Belgian or German IPA (with Belgian yeast and German hops respectively), black IPA (dark) or session IPA (less alcohol)

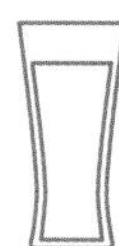

HANDKÄSE CHEESE WITH WIND MUSIC

INGREDIENTS
Serves 4

60 ml (2 fl oz/¼ cup) red ale
1 tablespoon honey
1 tablespoon beer vinegar or aromatic vinegar
3 tablespoons olive oil
1 teaspoon linseed oil
a few rocket (arugula) leaves
400 g (14 oz) handkäse cheese with caraway seeds
1 bunch radishes
1 small red onion
salt
wholegrain bread slices, to serve

Handkäse cheese *is a sour milk cheese produced in Germany. It is available in German delis or speciality cheese shops.*

'Handkäse cheese with wind music' is the classic dish from vineyard restaurants in Hesse, in which handkäse cheese is marinated in white wine, onions and vinegar. The brewery version with beer is clearly a Franconian–Bavarian creation, but likewise has the makings of a classic.

PREPARATION
20 minutes

METHOD

Make a vinaigrette by stirring together the ale, honey, beer vinegar, olive oil and linseed oil. Wash the rocket and spin-dry.

Cut the handkäse cheese into thin slices. Wash and dry the radishes and cut into thin slices or use a mandoline. Peel the red onion and cut into strips.

Mix all the ingredients except the salt and bread with the vinaigrette and season lightly with salt. Arrange the rocket, radish and onion on wholegrain bread to serve.

BEER STYLES: Red ales, wheat or normal bock.

SPECIAL RECOMMENDATION: Feierabendbier by Spencer Brewery, Massachusetts, USA. What could match better to a dish as German as this one than a typical German-style pilsener? Spencer Brewery is also the first and only brewing Trappist monastery in the United States.

Handkäse cheese with wind music

Pickled eggs

PICKLED EGGS

These eggs, pickled with herbs and onions in mildly acidic vinegar and spicy liquid, used to be considered fortifying pub food. There was always a well-filled glass standing in the hungerturm *(hunger tower), a glass display cabinet also housing bread and dripping, pickled gherkins and meatballs. Isn't it time to revive this beautiful tradition?*

INGREDIENTS

Makes 12

12 eggs
50 g (1¾ oz) salt, plus an extra pinch for cooking
150 ml (5 fl oz) beer vinegar, white wine vinegar or aromatic vinegar, plus an extra splash for cooking
80 g (2¾ oz) sugar
2 bay leaves
1 tablespoon mustard seeds
1 teaspoon caraway seeds
2 onions
4 summer savoury sprigs, or 3 thyme sprigs
4 tarragon sprigs
butter, to serve
24 pumpernickel rounds
mustard, to serve

PREPARATION

25 minutes (plus cooling time)

METHOD

Pierce the eggshells and cook the eggs in salted water with the extra splash of vinegar for 10–12 minutes. Set aside in cold water to cool.

In a saucepan, mix 1 litre (34 fl oz) water with the sugar, 50 g (1¾ oz) salt, 150 ml (5 fl oz) beer vinegar, bay leaves, mustard seeds and caraway seeds, and bring to the boil. Cut the onions into thin strips, add to the water and boil for 5 minutes. Add the whole sprigs of summer savoury and tarragon, then bring to the boil again.

Peel the eggs and stack in screw-top or clip-top preserving jars that have been sterilised in hot water. Pour over the hot pickling liquid and seal, then allow to cool.

Serve the eggs on buttered, lightly salted pumpernickel rounds with the mustard.

BEER STYLES: Different beer styles strengthen and match the taste of the eggs.

SPECIAL RECOMMENDATION: Braumeister Pils by Victory Brewing Company, Pennsylvania, USA – because something as German as pickled eggs deserves a pils with German hop varieties like Tettnang and Spalter Select.

FERAL
BREWING COMPANY
www.feralbrewing.com.au

SWAN VALLEY, AUSTRALIA

FERAL BREWING COMPANY

THE COUNTRY IDYLL

On the western rim of Australia, about a 40-minute drive from Perth and lying in the scenic Swan Valley, is the headquarters of the most award-winning craft-beer brewery in Australia – the Feral Brewing Company. A small hidden culinary jewel.

You have to imagine Brendan Varis as a deeply happy man: extremely relaxed, he's very successfully making what he loves – beer – surrounded by people who seem to be more good friends than fellow workers. And all this in an idyllic place that couldn't look more peaceful. His recipe for success? 'We don't look at what the others do, but simply brew the beer we'd most like to drink ourselves!'

The taste and curiosity of the founder and his head brewer are obviously wide-ranging, because their list offers more than 25 different beers. Sixteen of these are available to try on tap at the headquarters. The variety is an integral part of the Feral concept: 'Otherwise it would be like saying: "Hey, I've got fantastic vegetables here, it's all broccoli!" Brendan grins. Nevertheless, Feral allows itself the luxury of not bottling the majority of its beer. If you want to get to know the whole breadth of its magnificent beers, you have to make your way to the quiet Swan Valley.

Probably the best-known beer from Feral does, however, also come in a bottle: the multi-award-winning best Australian beer of 2011 and 2012, Hop Hog – an American-style IPA. Both during the brewing process and during maturation, it's strongly hopped with American aromatic hops. In the Feral repertoire, though, there are also strong beers, such as the 10 per cent barley wine Razorback or the chocolate-espresso-tasting Russian imperial stout Boris. The authentic-style witbier Feral White is fermented with 50 per cent wheat malt and 50 per cent barley malt – using Belgian yeast, orange peel and coriander. Feral proudly claims it's 'The best use of wheat since the invention of sliced bread!'

Of all the beers, it's probably Watermelon Warhead that in its way perfectly unites Brendan's nature and his beers. The name refers to a dearly loved sour candy from his childhood, the style reflects his great passion for sour beer, and the recipe is – like everything at Feral – creative and unconventional. A Berliner weisse, together with watermelons from the Swan Valley, are matured for six months in chardonnay casks. Sour beers really are his greatest passion. And so beers have arisen like the one brewed spontaneously with local Swan

Valley yeasts and matured in barrels, Funky Junky; or José Gosé – as its name suggests, a mildly salted gose.

The names are crucial. The name of the brewery itself indicates, just like the wild boar on its logo, the company's direction. Here people are unrestrained, free-spirited and wild. Beers are called Karma Chameleon or Barrique O'Karma (both black IPAs) and mirror the predominant way of life in the west: really laid back. The best proof of this is the quality testing and finding names for new Feral creations. They occur as a rule on a Friday afternoon: Brendan and his congenial master brewer and friend Will Irving get themselves, with the help of a jug, in that certain creative mood that seems necessary for finding suitable names. New beers only reach the market when they've also passed the four-jug test: 'When after four jugs we still want to have another one straight away, we assume our beer has the right balance,' Brendan laughs.

Beside the names, the creativity of the brewing recipes is second to none. 'I'm a big fan of the theory that brewing is 50 per cent knowledge and 50 per cent art,' he says, 'and I think at Feral we hit that mark pretty precisely!' Beers like Nan's Driving, an Earl Grey–seasoned amber ale with low alcohol, demonstrate an unlimited joy in experimentation, along with a good dose of humour.

What strikes you straight away at Feral, apart from the unbelievably relaxed atmosphere, is the high value people in the Swan Valley place on the quality of food. Because the Feral Brewing headquarters isn't just a brewery, it's also a total culinary work of art. The restaurant and herb and vegetable garden are an integral part of the Feral experience. Food here is much more than a mere necessary add-on to line the stomachs of the beer drinkers. The food is cooked *with* and *to suit* beer. As with, for example, the beef ribs or the beer-braised rabbit. Or with the seemingly simple combination of an outstanding Spanish chorizo with the Feral IPA Hop Hog: 'The sharpness of the chorizo dampens the bitterness and brings the fruit aromas of the hops more to the fore,' says Brendan. This pairing lifts both – food and drink – once again to a new, almost animated level.

'The first year we earned most of our money with the food,' he reports, and explains that the brewery has only been able to support itself from brewing alone for the past three years. But that's always improving. At any rate, the craft-beer sector of the total Australian beer market now makes up 10 per cent. A market share – and sales volume – of almost American proportions, that at the moment German proponents of a sophisticated brewing culture can only dream of. In Western Australia, by comparison, Feral has for some time been sharing its success in a brand-new 5,000 litre (1,320 gallon) brewing plant with craft-beer colleagues from Nail Brewing, and at the moment is also building a warehouse for barrel-matured beers that will accommodate 800 barrels of 400 litres (105 gallons) each. The old, small brewhouse in the picturesque headquarters has returned to country life but is also still regularly used – for the 'funky brews', as Brendan puts it – strong and sour beers – or for the next bold experiment that takes place under the sign of the wild boar.

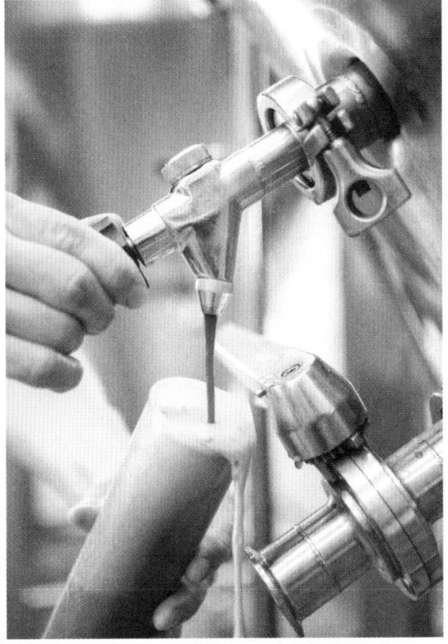

WHEN AFTER FOUR JUGS WE STILL WANT TO HAVE ANOTHER ONE STRAIGHT AWAY, WE ASSUME OUR BEER HAS THE RIGHT BALANCE.

#feralbrewhouse
TUSK

FERAL
PALE ALE
HOG

BREWPUB
SERIES
KNUCKLES
COFFEE IPA

BREWPUB
SERIES
WATERMELON
WARHEAD
BERLINER WEISSE

BREWPUB
SERIES
DRINK FRESH
TUSK
20TH MARCH 15
IIPA
9.8%

HAVING FUN – THAT'S IT, THAT'S WHAT BREWING CRAFT BEER IS ALL ABOUT.

SPRATS ON BLINI WITH BEETROOT SALAD AND TROUT ROE

INGREDIENTS

Makes 18 small blini

Beetroot salad

150 g (5½ oz) cooked beetroot (beets)
1 French shallot
1–2 teaspoons white wine vinegar, aromatic vinegar or apple cider vinegar
1 teaspoon caraway oil or nut oil
1 teaspoon olive oil
salt

Blini

2 eggs
250 ml (8½ fl oz/1 cup) beer
175 g (6 oz) plain (all-purpose) flour
175 g (6 oz) buckwheat flour
salt
oil, for frying

To serve

150 g (5½ oz) sour cream
18 Kiel sprats
50 g (1¾ oz) red trout roe

*

Kiel sprats
is the name of the small North Sea and Baltic herrings smoked over beechwood, which were traditionally sold in small wooden boxes. True seamen consume the sparkling gold fish whole, with head and tail. The rule for landlubbers: the soft crunchy bones should always be eaten.

These buckwheat pancakes arrive on the plate hot and fluffy, with smoked fish, cool sour cream, trout roe and beetroot (beet). And if you close your eyes in enjoyment while chewing, you can hear the roar of the Baltic Sea.

PREPARATION

About 90 minutes

METHOD

For the beetroot salad: Finely dice the beetroot. Peel and finely dice the shallots. Mix all the ingredients with the vinegar and oils and toss. Season with salt.

For the blini: Separate the eggs and mix the yolks with the beer. Sift the flours and mix with the yolk mixture to make smooth batter. Set aside for 10 minutes to rise. Beat the egg whites with a pinch of salt in a mixing bowl with the whisk of an electric mixer until stiff, then fold into the batter. Season the batter lightly with salt.

Preheat the oven to 80 °C (180 °F) and put in an ovenproof serving platter. Heat 2–3 tablespoons oil in a large non-stick frying pan. Drop 1–2 tablespoons of the batter into the oil for each blini, working in batches and spacing them comfortably, and cook for 2 minutes over medium heat. Turn them over and cook for another 2 minutes or until golden brown. Quickly drain finished blini on paper towel, then keep them warm on the platter in the oven. Repeat with the remaining batter, adding more oil as necessary.

Top the blinis with the soured cream, beetroot, sprats and trout roe, then serve immediately.

TIP: This dish also tastes great with any other sort of smoked fish.

BEER STYLES: Beers tasting strongly of roasted malt, such as black beer, stout and porter. Alternatively, try unfruity sour beer.

SPECIAL RECOMMENDATION: Viking Gose by The Monarchy (see the profile on page 175), brewed with a healthy shot of smoked malt. The salt, sourness and smoke in this beer form an aromatic accord that goes perfectly with the sprats and beetroot.

Sprats on blinis with beetroot salad and trout roe

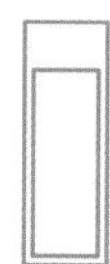

BEER PIZZA WITH SAUERKRAUT, REMOUDOU CHEESE AND MARJORAM CREAM

INGREDIENTS
Serves 4–6

Base
500 g (1 lb 2 oz/3⅓ cups) plain (all-purpose) flour, plus extra for dusting
125 g (4½ oz) dark wheat beer
20 g (¾ oz) salt
5 g (¼ oz) fresh yeast

Topping
285 g (10 oz) tinned sauerkraut
1 tablespoon olive oil, plus extra for drizzling
1 teaspoon sugar
salt
50 g (1¾ oz) cream cheese
100 g (3½ oz) sour cream
½ teaspoons caraway seeds
2 marjoram sprigs
300 g (10½ oz) remoudou cheese*
pepper
2 spring onions (scallions)

*

Remoudou
is a tangy washed-rind soft cheese, which comes originally from Belgium but is now also made in Allgäu in southern Germany. Also suitable are the reasonably closely related limburger, munster, taleggio and Reblochon cheeses.

The matured dough is already made with beer, but this tasty pizza with spring onions (scallions), sauerkraut and cheese also tastes best . . . with beer!

PREPARATION

45 minutes (plus 24 hours for the dough to rest)

METHOD

For the base: Mix 300 g (10½ oz/2 cups) of the flour with the beer, salt, 75 ml (2½ fl oz) cold water and the finely crumbled yeast to form a smooth batter. Cover and set aside to rest for 20 minutes.

Using an electric mixer with the dough hook, knead the mixture for 3 minutes. Gradually knead in the remaining flour. Knead for a further 2 minutes. Cover the soft dough and leave to rest for 20 minutes.

Turn the dough out onto a floured bench, dust with flour and knead into a ball with floured hands. Halve, seal in two airtight containers and refrigerate for 24 hours to mature.

For the topping: Drain the sauerkraut and mix with the olive oil, sugar and a little salt. Mix the cream cheese with the sour cream until smooth. Season with salt. Gently crush or roughly chop the caraway seeds. Pick the marjoram leaves and fold with the caraway seeds into the cream cheese mixture. Slice the remoudou as thinly as possible.

Preheat the oven as high as it will go. Working on a floured bench with floured fingers, form the mature base dough into four to six flatcakes with higher rims. Place over a floured fist and pull into pizza size and shape, then lay on a floured baking sheet.

Spread each base with the cream cheese and cream mixture, then divide the sauerkraut and remoudou between them. Season with pepper, then drizzle with a little olive oil. Bake on the bottom shelf at 220–250°C (430–480°F) for 12–15 minutes (at 220°C/430°F) or 8–12 minutes (at 250°C/480°F) until crisp. Cut the spring onion into thin slices on the diagonal and scatter over the pizza before serving.

BEER STYLES: Well-hopped beers such as pilsner or kölsch.

SPECIAL RECOMMENDATION: Pivo Hoppy Pils from Firestone Walker Brewing Company, California, USA. A pils hoppy enough to pair with the strong and intense elements of the pizza.

Beer pizza with sauerkraut, remoudou cheese and marjoram cream

I FIRST GOT TO KNOW REAL VARIETY IN HOPS IN BELGIUM

PETTING, BAVARIA

PRIVATE LANDBRAUEREI SCHÖNRAM

THE HOP VIRTUOSO

In the middle of Upper Bavaria, close to the border with Austria, sits Schönram, an idyllic town only 8 kilometres (5 miles) from the Alps. There lies a brewery that brewed a beer that in 2014 was crowned best pilsner in the world – and brewed by a man born in America.

Having a truly Bavarian-sounding voice with a deep sonorous bass – whoever hears Eric Toft speak for the first time doesn't catch on that with this master brewer of the small but excellent brewery in Petting they're not dealing with a native. At least for those not from Bavaria, Toft sounds absolutely authentic – including his use of specifically Bavarian vocabulary, such as *kraxeln* (clambering) when the conversation turns to the nearby mountains.

In fact, though, the head brewer at the Schönramer brewery is American-born – originally coming to Bavaria to train as a brewer in the Weihenstephan brewery with the plan of then returning to his homeland. Instead he stayed in Bavaria and has since – apart from a few years in Belgium – made it his home, perfectly assimilating right down to his traditional Bavarian *Trachtenjanker* (alpine coat). That he of all people has made Bavaria his home is no accident according to Toft. 'I have the mountain mentality,' he laughs and refers to his background in Wyoming, which he calls the 'Bavaria of America'.

What has certainly also played a role, apart from this mentality, is his proximity to the farming area that grows the basic ingredient of beer that Toft understands so subtly and discerningly, as only a few people in Germany do: hops. For example, in his multi-award-winning pilsner, which was recently named the world's best of its style in the World Beer Cup 2014, 'for that we use exclusively aromatic hops,' Toft reveals. The bitterness experienced is thus noticeably weaker than in factory pilsners – although the actual amount is analytically speaking the same. The large amount of other aromatics in his hops clothes the bitter alpha acid in, as it were, a soft coat – the bitterness is still present but it has a milder effect on the senses. Late additions of hops and the fully fermented, dry style of this beer are another thing they do to ensure a remarkably quaffable, balanced beer with great aromatic depth.

When you speak to Toft about hops and their meaning for Schönramer's beers, you notice straight away the intensity with which he dedicates himself to the theme. 'Terroir is a passion for me,' he explains – using a concept that's more at home in the wine world. There, terroir is the identity-giving origin of a wine. But why shouldn't soil structure and composition, microclimate and growing method also leave similarly clear traces in the world of hops?

Toft's original studies in geology and geophysics are possibly another reason for the strong meaning he attributes to origins. 'I know exactly where my hops grow,' he says, and reports that he still travels every year after the harvest to see the hop farmers and work with them to choose the candidate hops the brewery could use. Each hop farm is tested individually and of course 'blind', in other words without knowing where the hops being tried come from. 'Nevertheless, 90 per cent of the ones I select are from the same position – which speaks clearly for the importance of terroir also with hops,' he explains, not without a certain undertone of pride.

The care he dedicates to this subject is also a reaction to changing market conditions, because the worldwide craft-beer boom and consequent drastic rise in demand for aromatic hops has had unpleasant side effects in Germany. 'Six years ago we still got good hops from the USA for our pale ale and IPA, but now you can only get sixth- or seventh-rate ones from there,' Toft complains. The inevitable consequence is a categorical turn towards hops from Germany – including for specialist beers.

His favourite types are regional classics like Hallertauer, Hersbrucker or Tettnanger, despite his love for the hop family having been kindled in another place entirely. During his studies at Weihenstephan, the quality of the raw materials played as good as no role: 'there it was only ever about efficiency,' he explains. 'I only mutated into a hop fetishist in Belgium' – you can see in the enthusiastic way Topf talks about the use of hops and yeast there what an impression on him that time made.

It stands to reason that someone who, through a period of about two years in Belgium, came to understand the clearly more relaxed and freer approach to brewing outside Germany, developed the necessary knowledge to respond to the German Purity Law. But to him this verdict, often much maligned in craft-beer circles, is an incentive rather than a limitation. For example, in attempting to brew an 'authentic' Belgian triple, while conforming to the Purity Law, is actually impossible, because for this style an addition of sugar is obligatory – but this is forbidden in Germany. 'A thing like that spawns creativity,' Toft says.

For five years, Schönramer has also been brewing, besides traditional Bavarian styles like wheat beer, helles, pilsner and the remarkably quaffable Saphir Bock – which was originally inspired by a Belgian triple – innovative styles from the craft-beer domain. Ale, IPA and imperial stout are on this list, as is a fine quartet of stouts matured in wooden barrels of different origin – sherry, single-malt whisky, port and bourbon. A seasonal highlight is Grünhopfen Pils (green hop pilsner), brewed with fresh, undried hops. All of them are likewise brewed exclusively with German hops. 'With these beers I wanted to show what's also possible within the framework of the Purity Law,' Toft says. Their success proves him right: when we visited, a new storage tank had just been installed – testimony in steel to the great success Schönramer is also enjoying in the craft-beer scene.

Die Bedienung
des Aufzuges
ist nur dem Brau-
er Kellnerge=
stattet.

Müller
84069 Inkofen

WITHOUT CLEVER RAW MATERIALS I CAN'T MAKE CLEVER BEER.

15
16

Bacon jam

WESTERN BREAKFAST WITH BACON JAM

Bacon is a tasty all-purpose weapon in the kitchen and can even be made into a 'jam' – and it really goes with everything: on burgers and pizzas, in pasta dishes, with jacket potatoes, and in stews and sauces. Or equally with a western breakfast: on English muffins, with fried eggs and a pickled gherkin salad.

PREPARATION
25 minutes

METHOD

For the bacon jam: Finely dice the bacon. Peel and finely dice the onions. In a large frying pan, stirring, render the bacon, then cook it in its own fat until golden brown. Add the onions and fry, stirring, until golden brown. Peel the garlic and stir in with the paprika. Deglaze with the beer and bring to the boil, then add the golden syrup and balsamic vinegar. Bring to the boil and cook, uncovered, for 6–8 minutes, until thick. Use immediately or pour hot into sterilised screw-top jars, seal and leave to cool. Once open, bacon jam keeps in the jar in the refrigerator for 4 weeks.

For the western breakfast: Finely dice the shallot, finely chop the dill and mix both with the gherkin slices. Mix in the gherkin pickling liquid and olive oil. Arrange on plates.

Halve and toast the muffins. Heat the butter in a frying pan over low heat and fry the eggs. Season with salt. Spread the muffins with the bacon jam and serve with the eggs and gherkin salad.

BEER STYLES: Beers with strongly toasty aromatics, like porter, stout and imperial stout, or high-alcohol IPAs and smoked beers.

SPECIAL RECOMMENDATION: Aecht Schlenkerla Rauchbier Märzen by Brauerei Heller, Bamberg, Germany – because nothing matches better with bacon than the intense smokiness of a beer brewed with smoked malt.

INGREDIENTS
Serves 4

Bacon jam
500 g (1 lb 2 oz) streaky bacon without gristle
500 g (1 lb 2 oz) onions
1–2 garlic cloves
large pinch of smoked paprika
200 ml (7 fl oz) dark beer
3 tablespoons golden or maple syrup
1 tablespoon balsamic vinegar

Western breakfast
1 French shallot
2 dill sprigs
60 g (2 oz) Danish pickled gherkins, drained and sliced
1–2 tablespoons gherkin pickling liquid
2 tablespoons olive oil
4 English muffins*
20 g (¾ oz) butter
4 eggs
salt
60 g (2 oz/¼ cup) bacon jam

*

English muffins
lie somewhere between toast and bread rolls. They taste good warm and cold, and in England they are eaten at breakfast, halved and toasted. They are great with butter and marmalade, cheese, ham, sausage – and, of course, bacon jam!

Mustard kidneys with baby spinach on toast

MUSTARD KIDNEYS WITH BABY SPINACH ON TOAST

The word has probably got out that animals aren't just made of steaks, but that offal dishes can shine with new tastes and aromas hasn't got around so well. The following recipe recommends itself to curious beginners and gourmets alike.

PREPARATION

30 minutes

METHOD

Clean the kidney pieces, remove the fat and white core, and halve the larger pieces. Peel and finely dice the onion and garlic. Heat the oil in a large non-stick frying pan over medium heat, then fry the kidneys for 3 minutes.

Add half the onion and garlic, and cook for a further 2 minutes. Sprinkle over the sugar. Deglaze with the beer and boil, uncovered, for 1 minute. Pour in the stock and bring to the boil. Cook for 2–3 minutes until thick. Stir in the mustards and half the butter. Season with salt and balsamic vinegar, and keep warm.

Wash the spinach leaves in lukewarm water and spin dry. In a saucepan, melt the remaining butter with the remaining onion and garlic until foaming and cook until the onion is transparent. Stir in the spinach and allow to wilt. Season with salt. Toast the bread and divide the spinach between the slices. Top with the kidneys and serve immediately.

BEER STYLES: Malt-flavoured, not too strong beers. Altbier, amber ale, märzen, dunkles.

SPECIAL RECOMMENDATION: Kill Your Darlings by Thornbridge Brewery, Derbyshire, England. A malty, slightly sweet amber lager with just the perfect dose of hops to match with spinach and kidney.

INGREDIENTS

Serves 4

400 g (14 oz) calf livers (order from your butcher)
1 onion
1 garlic clove
3 tablespoons olive oil
pinch of sugar
50 ml (1¾ fl oz) beer
100 ml (3½ oz) beef stock
1 teaspoon German mustard
1 teaspoon wholegrain mustard
40 g (1½ oz) cold butter
salt
1–2 drops balsamic vinegar
200 g (7 oz/4 cups) baby English spinach
4 slices white bread

TOAST-FLAVOURED

IMPERIAL STOUT

Coffee and chocolate notes marry with malty sweetness and hop bitterness. The result: an almost cryptic depth. This finer and stronger variant of the dockworkers' beer, porter, was once exported as far as the Russian court of Catherine the Great. So dark it's opaque, this high-alcohol brew has the complexity otherwise reserved only for great wines.

ORIGIN	England
CHARACTER	Malty/toasty and very complex
FERMENTATION	As a rule top-fermented
ALCOHOL CONTENT	8–12% Vol.
DRINKING TEMP	11–15°C (52–59°F)
BEST GLASS	Stout glass
EXAMPLES	de Molen's Hel & Verdoemenis, BrewDog's Tokyo, Samuel Smith's Imperial Stout
RECIPES	Liptauer (p. 58), Beetroot with Pancetta (p. 70), Rib-eye Steak with Balsamic Butter Sauce (p. 170)
VARIANTS	Stout, porter (weaker), oatmeal stout, coffee or chocolate porter or stout, milk stout (with unfermentable milk sugar), Baltic porter (bottom-fermented)

CHEF-STYLE LIPTAUER CHEESE SPREAD

INGREDIENTS
Serves 4–6

100 g (3½ oz) feta
250 g (9 oz/1 cup) creamy quark
100 g (3½ oz) cream cheese
1 tablespoon beer
1 tablespoon cornichon pickling water
1 garlic clove
1 teaspoon caraway seeds
1 tablespoon sweet paprika, plus extra to serve
salt
hot paprika
1 onion
1 potato, cooked the day before, peeled
4 cornichons
1 flat-leaf (Italian) parsley sprig
1 tablespoon capers, rinsed and squeezed dry
a little canola or linseed oil

*
Liptauer
*is a cheesemaking method originally from Slovakia–Hungary that uses quark-like rennet cheese made from sheep's and cow's milk (*bryndza*), mixed with cream, butter and various spices. The spreading cheese is today considered a cultural treasure in Hungary, Austria, Slovakia and the Czech Republic. In Bavaria, liptauer is part of any decent tea break, and there's hardly a beer garden that doesn't offer this tasty cream, best of all on crisp* brezn *(dialect for 'pretzel').*

With a little makeover rustic liptauer can be turned into an elegant cream fit for the best company. Nevertheless, there's no need to serve the accompanying beer in Champagne flutes.*

PREPARATION
20 minutes

METHOD

Finely crumble the feta and mix with the quark, cream cheese, beer and cornichon pickling water until smooth. Peel the garlic and dice finely, crush the caraway seeds finely with a mortar and pestle and mix them both in with the sweet paprika. Season the liptauer with salt and a little hot paprika.

Peel the onion, cut into thick rings and colour on one side in a non-stick frying pan without oil (this creates a lovely smoked aroma!). Season with salt and set aside. Finely dice the potato. Slice the cornichons thinly. Pick the parsley leaves.

Arrange the cream on a plate or platter and garnish with the potato, cornichons, capers, onion and parsley. Sprinkle over some sweet paprika and serve drizzled with a little oil.

BEER STYLES: Served with bread, this classic spread goes with most beers, but especially with strong and dark beers such as strong ales or imperial ales.

SPECIAL RECOMMENDATION: Imperial Brown Stout London 1856 from The Kernel, Bermondsey, England. A mighty intense stout full of complex flavours.

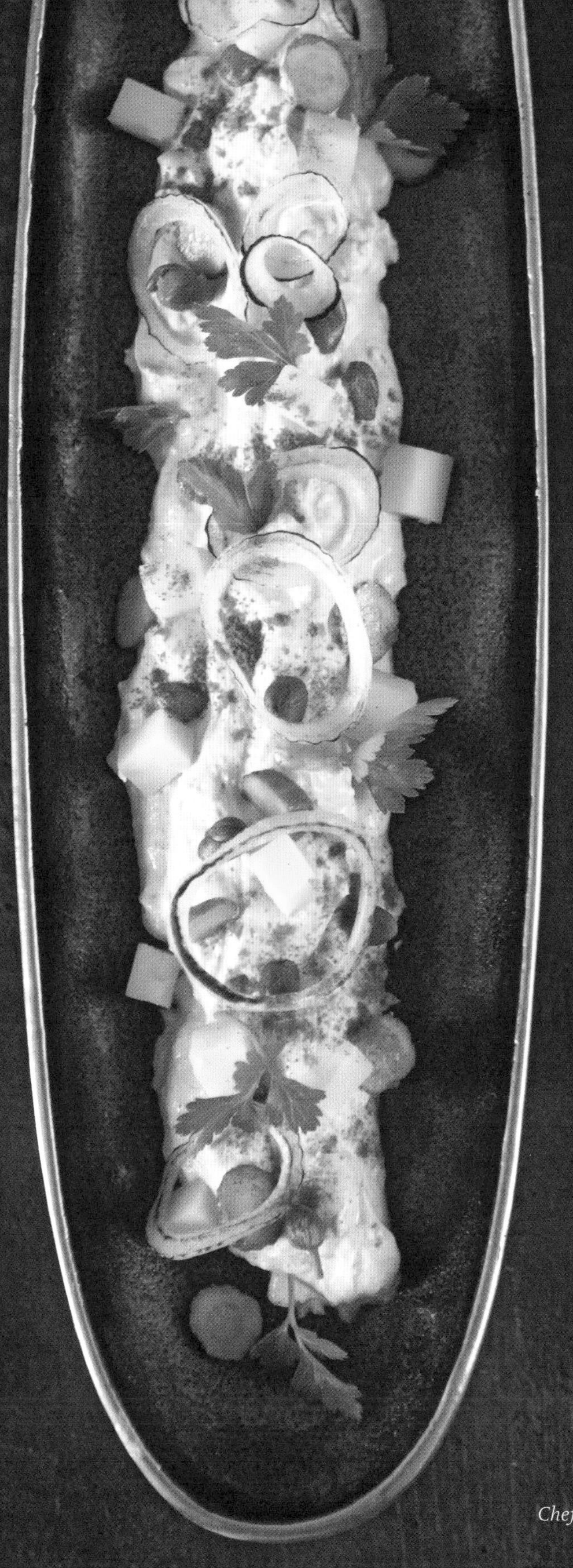

Chef-style liptauer cheese spread

Kepta duona

KEPTA DUONA

I first tasted the original version of this, probably the best beer snack in the world, in a Lithuanian restaurant in Hamburg. With it they served, in large pot-bellied glasses, ice-cold, ruby-red baltijos beer from the Lithuanian brewery Švyturys – the whole evening I ordered almost nothing else.

INGREDIENTS

Serves 6

200 g (7 oz) spreadable creamy cheese
100 g (3½ oz) very ripe runny cow's milk cheese (e.g. munster, époisses, chaource)
2 tablespoons beer
6 slices rye bread
60 ml (2 fl oz/¼ cup) oil
1 garlic clove
20 g (¾ oz) butter
salt

PREPARATION

15 minutes

METHOD

Combine the processed cheese, cow's milk cheese and beer in a saucepan and melt over low heat while mixing constantly with an electric mixer on the lowest setting.

Cut the rye bread into strips like chips (fries). Heat the oil in a frying pan with the halved garlic clove, until the garlic begins to brown slightly. Remove the garlic halves from the pan, add the bread strips and fry them in the garlic oil until golden brown and crisp. Toss through the butter, season with salt, drizzle over the cheese sauce and serve with beer.

BEER STYLES: Pale and red ales, rotbier, smoked beer, märzen . . . and any other good beer.

SPECIAL RECOMMENDATION: Naturally, the Švyturys Baltijos from Lithuania that inspired this recipe. A lighter, perhaps more readily available alternative would be Oktoberfest by Sierra Nevada, California, USA, the last version brewed in collaboration with Mahrs Bräu, Bamberg, Germany.

PUMPKIN RÖSTIS WITH FRIED DUCK LIVERS AND MANDARINS

INGREDIENTS
Serves 4

Pumpkin röstis
600 g (1 lb 5 oz) jap pumpkin (winter squash)
2 French shallots
1 tablespoon plain (all-purpose) flour
1 teaspoon cornflour (cornstarch)
salt
freshly ground white pepper
2 tablespoons clarified butter (ghee)

Duck liver with mandarins
2 mandarins
300 g (10½ oz) duck livers
3 tablespoons olive oil
20 g (¾ oz) butter
2 marjoram sprigs
salt
pepper

What to do with all those pumpkins in autumn! These crispy röstis made from jap pumpkins are a fabulous solution, and are a real discovery in combination with the tasty duck livers and sweet mandarins.

PREPARATION
30 minutes

METHOD

For the pumpkin röstis: Remove the seeds from the pumpkin, cut into large pieces and grate with the skin on (this is particularly easy with a food processor). Peel and finely dice the shallots, then mix into the grated pumpkin. Mix the flour and cornflour together, then fold into the pumpkin mixture and season with salt and white pepper.

Preheat the oven to 50 °C (120 °F) with an ovenproof platter inside it. Heat the clarified butter in a frying pan, then fry about eight röstis in two batches. Drop portions of the rösti mixture into the hot fat and press flat. Fry for 2–3 minutes until golden brown, then flip them carefully using two spatulas and fry on the other side for 2–3 minutes. Remove from the pan, drain on paper towel and keep warm on the platter in the oven.

For the duck liver with mandarins: Peel the mandarins and separate into segments. Remove the skin and white core from the duck livers, rinse in cold water and dry with paper towel. Heat the olive oil in a frying pan, add the livers and fry for 2 minutes on each side.

Add the mandarin segments and butter to the pan and fry everything together for a further 2 minutes. Roughly chop the marjoram and toss through. Season with salt and pepper. Immediately serve the liver and mandarin with the röstis on warmed plates.

BEER STYLES: Pale ale or IPA, pumpkin ale.

SPECIAL RECOMMENDATION: Post Road Pumpkin Ale by the craft-beer legend Brooklyn Brewery, New York, a seasonal specialty brewed in the United States only during pumpkin season. The not very cheap but extremely exquisite gourmet alternative is Hofstettner's Iced IPA G'froren's (see p. 81), a light, sweet, strongly hopped eisbock with almost 13 per cent alcohol.

Pumpkin röstis with fried duck livers and mandarins

I LIKE THE PHYSICAL ASPECTS OF BREWING.

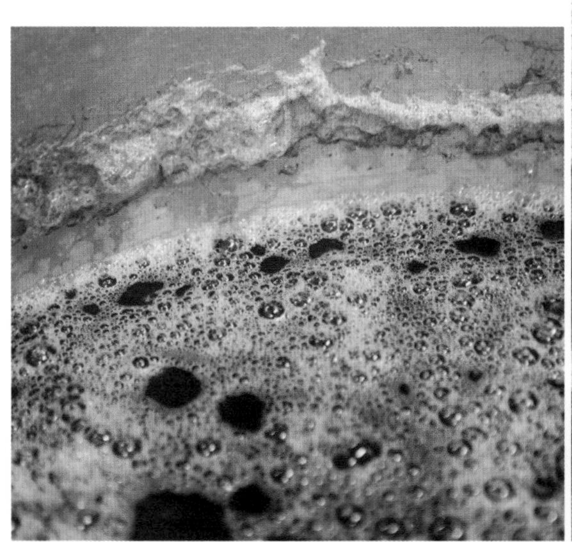

LONDON, UK

THE KERNEL BREWERY

THE PURIST

Plain brown paper with the brewery name, beer style, hops used and alcohol content in black. A beer label can hardly be simpler than at Kernel. This minimalism says a lot about Evin O'Riordain's attitude to brewing: concentrating on basic, uncompromisingly good beer.

The London suburb Bermondsey, south of the Thames, has in recent years gathered in the picturesque arches of its railway viaduct an exquisite collection of different food and drink producers and retailers. Under the name Spa Terminus, all are united in a passionate dedication to what they do and to an unconditional striving for quality. A branch of the royal-warrant-holding butcher O'Shea's is there, as is the bakery of the nose-to-tail eating pioneer and reformer of British cooking, Fergus Henderson. Cheese producers are also there, as are various remarkably knowledgeable organic wine sellers. Among many others, at number 11 is the brewery whose name always comes up whenever the conversation turns to the best craft-beer brewer of the British capital: the Kernel Brewery.

'Kernel' has many meanings but one of them is essence. Evin O'Riordain, the founder, couldn't have chosen a better name to characterise his beer philosophy. 'The brewery springs from the need to have more good beer,' says Kernel's website. 'Beer deserving of a certain attention. Beer that forces you to confront and consider what you are drinking.' You could hardly express its mission better.

O'Riordain first came across brewing in 2007 in New York, when he was there for Neal's Yard Dairy, a British cheese seller and producer, advising a customer on setting up a cheese business in Manhattan. For O'Riordain, New York was a kind of epiphany. 'It wasn't just the outstanding quality of the beer they had there,' he explains, 'it was just as much the way people there spoke about beer. They knew everything about it. Where the hops came from, where the malt came from, every detail! Just like at the time I could talk about cheese.' The passion, seriousness and respect people there devoted to the subject of beer would become the germ for Kernel.

Back in London again, O'Riordain took up homebrewing. The intensity with which he approached it led quickly to early success. The natural next step was founding the brewery. Since then Kernel has brewed three different groups of beers: pale ales and IPAs flavoured with American-style aromatic hops; then traditional British stouts and porter based on old, historical recipes;

I'D LIKE PEOPLE TO LISTEN NOT TO WHAT I HAVE TO SAY BUT RATHER TO WHAT THE BEER HAS TO SAY.

and finally sour beers partially fermented with wild yeasts and matured in barrels. The last of these especially are highly individual, thanks to some of the yeast originating from the brewery environment, which makes them particularly bound to the place where they're made.

One indication of the exceptionally good reputation Kernel has garnered in the European craft-beer scene is the fact that the brewery was among those selected by Jean van Roy of Cantillon for his Zwanze Day 2014 (see p. 119). 'We love what Cantillon makes, so it was a great honour to be allowed to be there,' Evin says. And it allowed him to analyse, very precisely, how different the brewing process there is in comparison to his own. 'Normally when you're brewing you're constantly busy avoiding things,' he says. Infections with unwanted yeast strains, for example, or the development of off flavours. At Cantillon, in contrast, they work with the environment rather than constantly fighting it, 'as if they were having a constructive conversation with it.' Even though this approach to beer isn't Evin O'Riordain's own, you can clearly hear in his voice how much the concept appeals to him.

As a rule Kernel brews sell incredibly quickly. Its enormous success and the simultaneous painful lack of space under the arches of Spa Terminus provide a rather limited degree of enjoyment. The brewery is now working at the upper limit of its capacity. But there's no question of Kernel becoming a gypsy brewer in order to increase production in a larger brewing plant. 'We've thought about it, but it's not really what we want to do,' Evin says. 'We simply like brewing too much for that!' The direct physical contact with the process of brewing is just as important to him as before, he says. 'That's why we do nothing else other than brewing.' The intensity with which O'Riordain says this leaves no doubt that the physical–sensory component is for him an indispensable part of his work.

Unfortunately, on the other side of the Channel very few bottles from Kernel are available. Because, as we said, no one in Bermondsey is worrying themselves with sales. Now and then the beers appear at craft-beer festivals on the Continent. The best advice, however, is to make your way, while visiting London – for craft-beer enthusiasts arguably the most interesting city in Europe at the moment – to Bermondsey on a Saturday between 9 am and 2 pm to buy a few bottles direct from the brewer. And then, since you're already in Bermondsey, perhaps buy a piece of two of outstanding cheese. Evin O'Riordain's recommendation is the combination of two representatives of traditional British cuisine: stilton and the Kernel's Imperial Brown, brewed to a recipe from 1856.

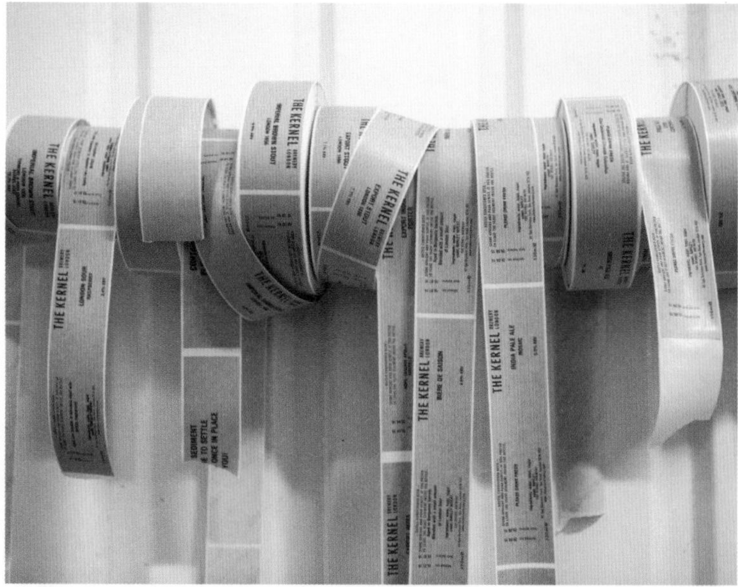
THE KERNEL
INDIA PALE ALE

MOHAWK
BLACK ROCKET
YEAR ROUND BEER
PORTER
BREWING COMPANY

US Cascade 2014
Alpha: 5.00%
Oil: 1.50%

THE ONLY THING THAT'S REALLY IMPORTANT IS WHAT'S IN THE BOTTLE.

BEETROOT WITH PANCETTA AND CARAMELISED WALNUTS

INGREDIENTS
Serves 4

500 g (1 lb 2 oz) small to medium beetroot (beets) (about 4)
salt
3 tablespoons sugar
2 tablespoons dark beer
20 g (3/4 oz) butter
20 walnuts
1 tablespoon beer vinegar
1 tablespoon balsamic vinegar
3 tablespoons apple juice
1 tablespoon honey
60 ml (2 fl oz/1/4 cup) olive oil
freshly ground black pepper
80 g (2 3/4 oz) very finely sliced pancetta*

*

Pancetta
is Italian pork belly bacon, often spiced with pepper and salted, and also available rolled as pancetta arrotolata, a round air-dried bacon. If you can't get pancetta, you can use coppa (see p. 29). It also works very well with bündnerfleisch or a mildly salted, local raw ham.

Warm marinated beetroot (beets) in an intense beer vinegar and balsamic vinaigrette, with airy-thin pancetta, sweet crisp walnuts and a hint of salt. It takes a little time to cook the beetroot, but otherwise this elegant appetiser is hardly any work. A perfect match for dark, malty beer.

PREPARATION
About 90 minutes

METHOD

Wash the beetroot and simmer in salted water for up to 60 minutes. When a skewer passes easily through the beetroot they are done.

Meanwhile, bring the sugar and beer to the boil in a frying pan until lightly caramelised. Melt in the butter, then add the walnuts and caramelise them for 1–2 minutes. Season lightly with salt and leave to cool on baking paper.

Make a vinaigrette by stirring together the beer vinegar, balsamic vinegar, apple juice, honey and olive oil, and season with salt and pepper.

Strain the beetroot and peel under cold water. Allow to cool a little, then slice thinly. Arrange on serving plates like carpaccio. Arrange the pancetta in the middle. Drizzle the beetroot with the vinaigrette, then scatter over the walnuts.

BEER STYLES: Dark and heavy malt-flavoured beers such as dark doppelbock or imperial stout.

SPECIAL RECOMMENDATION: Speedway Stout by AleSmith Brewing Company, San Diego, USA. Intense malt, dark chocolate, coffee and dried fruits are a perfect match for the earthy beetroot aroma. A (highly complex) match made in heaven!

Beetroot with pancetta and caramelised walnuts

Salad of three fried crucifers with smoked trout and lemon

SALAD OF THREE FRIED CRUCIFERS WITH SMOKED TROUT AND LEMON

When fried, cauliflower, broccoli and broccolini gain a nutty flavour and retain their bite. Tender smoked trout and a fresh lemon vinaigrette suit the vegetables perfectly, to make an exceptional winter salad that's both filling and enjoyable.

PREPARATION
20 minutes

METHOD

Cut the broccoli into small florets, then halve the florets. Slice the cauliflower. Halve the broccolini lengthways and trim off the end of the stems. Heat half the olive oil in a large non-stick frying pan over medium heat. Add the vegetables, and season with salt and add half the sugar. Fry, stirring, for 6–8 minutes.

For the vinaigrette, mix the lemon zest and juice with the orange juice, mustard, honey, remaining olive oil and linseed oil. Season with salt and the remaining pinch of sugar. Wash the mizuna and spin dry.

Break up the trout into bite-sized pieces. Mix the warm vegetables with the trout, mizuna and vinaigrette, then season to taste if needed with more salt or lemon juice.

BEER STYLES: Well-hopped pale ales or IPAs.

SPECIAL RECOMMENDATION: Dead Pony Pale Ale by BrewDog, Scotland. This ale, hopped in the style of a West Coast IPA, captivates with only 3.8 per cent alcohol and easy-drinking lightness, and leaves the crucifers, smoked trout and fruity marinated salad enough room.

INGREDIENTS
Serves 4

about 200 g (7 oz) each broccoli, cauliflower and broccolini*
90 ml (3 fl oz) olive oil
salt
2 pinches of sugar
grated zest and juice of ½ organic lemon
2 tablespoons orange juice
1 teaspoon mustard
1 teaspoon honey
1 teaspoon linseed oil
50 g (1¾ oz) mizuna**
200 g (7 oz) skinless smoked trout fillets

*

Broccolini,
with small florrets atop a long stem, broccolini is related to broccoli and was grown by the Ancient Romans.

**

Mizuna
This recipe should actually be called 'Salad of Four Crucifers', because this lettuce from Japan is actually from the same cabbage family. The gently serrated, decorative leave taste spicy and nutty, with a slight sourness. If you can't get mizuna, use frisée.

STRONGLY HOPPED

ALTBIER

Now only still available in the Lower Rhine region, but originally much more widespread. The name refers to the 'old' – that is top-fermented – brewing style, in contrast to the bottom-fermented pilsner that at the time was causing a furore. Apart from the regional competitor kölsch (which as a rule is milder and more quaffable but less complex), this is the only traditional top-fermented German beer style made with barley malt. Amber red or copper-coloured, with a strong bitterness and a malty body.

ORIGIN	Germany
CHARACTER	Strongly hopped with a malty base
FERMENTATION	Top-fermented
ALCOHOL CONTENT	4.5–5.5% Vol.
DRINKING TEMP	6–8°C (43–46°F)
BEST GLASS	Altbier glass
EXAMPLES	Uerige Alt, Uerige Sticke, Schumacher Alt, Schlüssel Alt
RECIPES	Apple and Scamorza Salad (p. 76), Cheeseburger (p. 144), Fried Black Sausage (p. 142), Mustard Kidneys (p. 55)
VARIANTS	Slightly sour altbiers such as the one from Münster or traditional adambier from Dortmund. Stronger brews such as sticke alt (6%) or doppelsticke alt (8.5%).

APPLE AND SMOKED SCAMORZA CHEESE SALAD WITH A MUSTARD AND DILL VINAIGRETTE

Fresh, raw apple, smoked cheese and a slightly sour tangy vinaigrette with mustard and dill notes invite a glass of beer.

INGREDIENTS
Serves 2–4

2 tablespoons naturally cloudy apple juice
1 tablespoon apple cider vinegar, beer vinegar or white wine vinegar
1 tablespoon honey
1 tablespoon wholegrain mustard
3 tablespoons olive oil
salt
150 g (5½ oz) mild smoked scamorza*
1 apple
2–3 dill sprigs

*

Scamorza
is a pear-shaped mozzarella that has been dried for a few days in the air. It is thus somewhat firmer than mozzarella and is sold lightly salted or also smoked over beechwood. It's recognisable from its 'noose', by which the cheese is hung in the air and/or over the smoke. The paler the scamorza, the more mildly it has been smoked. Also try this recipe with esrom or true mozzarella.

PREPARATION
15 minutes

METHOD

Make a vinaigrette by stirring together the apple juice, apple cider vinegar, honey, mustard and olive oil. Season with salt. Slice the scamorza as thinly as possible.

Core the apple with an apple-corer and slice into rings as thinly as possible.

Arrange the cheese and the apple rings on a platter in an alternating tile pattern. Finely pick the dill and scatter over. Drizzle with the vinaigrette.

TIP: A baguette or sourdough bread goes well with this dish.

BEER STYLES: A well-hopped beer with not too much alcohol, such as altbier, pale ale or session IPA.

SPECIAL RECOMMENDATION: India Hells Lager by Camden Town Brewery, England. A premium lager, hoppy enough to be a counterweight to the smoky scamorza and light enough to not dominate the fruitiness of the apple.

Apple and smoked scamorza cheese salad with a mustard and dill vinaigrette

Leek cooked in butter with bündnerfleisch and toasted nuts

LEEK COOKED IN BUTTER WITH BÜNDNERFLEISCH AND TOASTED NUTS

Addictive. Leek simmered in butter becomes wonderfully tender and almost melts in the mouth; the toasted hazelnuts take care of crispness, and the seasoned bündnerfleisch crowns this equally simple and wonderful dish.

PREPARATION
30 minutes

METHOD
Remove the first layer of outer leaves on the leeks, which won't be necessary for this dish (use them, for example, to make vegetable stock). Cut the leeks into 7 cm (2¾ in) lengths. Peel the garlic and cut in half. In a small, high-sided saucepan, melt the butter, add the garlic and season with salt. Lay the leek pieces in the pan, then cover and cook over medium heat in the butter for 20 minutes or until done.

Meanwhile, toast the hazelnut flakes in the oil in a frying pan until brown, season lightly with salt and remove to a plate. Remove the leek from the butter, arrange on prewarmed plates, and sprinkle each with 1–2 splashes of apple cider vinegar. Divide the hazelnuts and bündnerfleisch between them. Serve immediately.

TIP: This tastes great with coarse rye bread or a baguette.

BEER STYLES: Pale beers without too much hop bitterness, helles, lager, kölsch. Or even a mild pilsner.

SPECIAL RECOMMENDATION: A Bavarian or Franconian Helles, or for something a little more common, the Gorch Fock Helles by Three Floyds Brewing Company, Indiana, USA.

INGREDIENTS
Serves 4

4 thin young leeks
1 garlic clove
500 g (1 lb 2 oz) butter
salt
2 tablespoons flaked hazelnuts
1 teaspoon hazelnut oil, another nut oil or olive oil
a few splashes of apple cider vinegar
200 g (7 oz) bündnerfleisch**

*

Any wonderfully aromatic leek remaining in the saucepan will taste great on bread or with fish; is suitable for flavouring vegetable soups, pasta or rice; and can be served with boiled new potatoes.

**

Bündernerfleisch
Bündnerfleisch is a type of air-dried meat, made with lean beef that has been trimmed of any fat, then cured with salt and spices before drying.

ZU
WÜRZE
WASSER
ZU
L.A.RIEDINGER
BITTE!

HOFSTETTEN, AUSTRIA

LANDBRAUHAUS HOFSTETTEN

TRADITION AND INNOVATION

The estate itself was first mentioned in documents in 1229 and a brewery has been there since 1449. Presumably beer was brewed here from the beginning, but the even the later date is enough for an entry in the Guinness Book of Records *as the 'oldest brewery in Austria'.*

North of the Danube in Upper Austria lies the Mühlviertel region. Austria's oldest brewery has its headquarters there and, after an eventful history, it has been in the Krammer family for five generations. In the mid-1990s it shared the same fate as many smaller country breweries: quality problems led first to a loss of customers and then to such a deep crisis that the accountant, in view of the figures, finally advised closing the business. For Peter Krammer that was not an option. His alternative, after much consideration, was to do his homework, get the quality under control, and through individuality and innovation remove the brewery from competition with factory brands and win back customers.

Today, a short twenty years later, you have to admit that the plan has worked. More than fifteen different beers have since been brewed in Hofstetten and some even exported to America. Next to the old brewhouse from 1929 now stands a modern one with the brewing capacity to meet the enormously increased demand.

'In 1998 we needed a sign that would symbolise our change of direction,' says Peter Krammer about Hofstetten's most obvious innovative moment – a new look and feel for such an old brewery so rich in tradition. 'A friend who at the time had just started an agency designed it for me.' But naturally the innovation in Hofstetten wasn't confined to appealingly designed labels. The true innovations occurred outside the office. For example, in the form of the granitbock, open-fermented in granite troughs more than 200 years old and made sophisticated with glowing granite flavours. The technique comes from the days when not all brewers could afford metal brew kettles. Since at that time you couldn't heat a wooden tub with fire, they came up with the idea of putting hot stones in the liquid to heat it. One of the side effects is that some of the available sugar in the wort caramelises on the glowing surface – and thus also gives the wort, beside the typical caramel flavours, a certain residual sweetness that the yeast can't ferment.

Hofstetten's Honigbier (honey beer) and Honigbock are the result of a successful mixture of tradition and innovation. 'After our pumpkin beer it was my most creative beer,' he reports, and explains that enrichment with honey used to be very common in the area. The honey Krammer uses for his beer varies. The honey beer uses regional organic honey from the Hochland Imker (highland beekeeper) company. For the bock, which has a noticeably stronger honey flavour, he experiments anew each year with different-flavoured honeys. This creates multilayered, complex beers with notes, for example, of linden blossom or chestnut. For some time the innovation-loving Krammer has also been experimenting with laying his granitbock and honey bock in wooden barrels. Sometimes he uses calvados barrels for this maturation step, sometimes Italian red wine casks, which add wild *Brettanomyces* yeast to the beer and lend further depth and complexity to the already multilayered beers.

When you speak to Peter Krammer, he gives the impression of an almost overflowing creativity and an innovative spirit. We're talking about using an old, disused wooden tub as the possible basis for experiments with spontaneous fermentation. We discuss the impact of the yeasts and Krammer describes his experiments with open fermentation in basins left under apple and pear trees – with clearly discernible results. In general, the influence of different yeasts on the flavour profile of beers is woefully underestimated. The high oxygen injection from the old technique – which when brewing pilsner, for example, is rather undesirable – suits other styles much better. And the old brewhouse won't go unused either once the new building is completed.

The attachment to the region is also important for Peter Krammer. Together with other breweries and a barkeeper he founded the Bierviertel (beer quarter) initiative, which is committed to the preservation of the regional identification with brewing. At Hofstetten itself he has the Mühlviertler Bio-Bier (organic beer) in the works, which will be brewed with 100 per cent organic raw materials from the region. It demands a little persuasiveness to convince the four surrounding farmers to grow the necessary winter barley – old, traditional regional sorts. Since 2010, Hofstetten itself has also been producing the finest barley for brewing. The estate also owns about 14 hectares (35 acres) of cultivable land that, because it lies partially in a water conservation area, has already been farmed for a long time under organic conditions. The water for brewing the Hofstetten beers is also fed by springs arising from the very same water conservation area.

We could go on for a long time about Peter Krammer's beers – about his first craft wort for pumpkin beer, for example. The idea came from tasting pumpkin-flavoured sausages from a butcher he's since befriended. Or about G'froren's, his strongly hopped eisbock. Or his eloquent silence when he's asked whether after growing barley the logical step wouldn't be his own malt. One thing is certain: we will hear a lot about Hofstetten in the future.

COPYING A BEER IS THE STUPIDEST THING A BREWER CAN DO.

HONIGBIER

KHK

KÜBELBIER

GRANIT

Fried baby leeks with melted cheese and new potatoes

FRIED BABY LEEKS WITH MELTED CHEESE AND NEW POTATOES

The young leeks are lightly floured before frying, which makes them beautifully crispy. Only lightly salted, they accompany oven-melted cheese, along with boiled new potatoes. Happiness tastes this simple.

PREPARATION

25 minutes

METHOD

Preheat the oven to 150 °C (300 °F). Cook the whole potatoes in salted water with the caraway seeds for 15–20 minutes until soft.

Wash the leeks, trim the roots and cut off enough of the green ends for the leeks to fit in a frying pan. Cook in boiling salted water in a saucepan for 2 minutes, remove with a slotted spoon and transfer to cold water to cool. Drain on paper towel.

Heat the cheese in the oven for 6–10 minutes.

Meanwhile, toss the leeks in the flour and fry in hot olive oil in a frying pan, turning once. Season with salt, drain on paper towel and grind over pepper. Serve with the cheese and potatoes.

TIP: Baby leek goes very well as a side dish with raclette or fondue.

BEER STYLES: Well-hopped beers that aren't too high in alcohol, pilsner, hopfenweisse, session IPAs.

SPECIAL RECOMMENDATION: Reality Czeck by Moonlight Brewing Company, California, USA. A perfectly balanced Czech pilsner with floral and grassy hop in the aftertaste.

INGREDIENTS

Serves 4

800 g (1 lb 12 oz) new potatoes
salt
1 teaspoon caraway seeds
16 quite thick baby leeks
2 cheeses* (about 200 g/7 oz each)
1 tablespoon plain (all-purpose) flour
75 ml (2½ fl oz) olive oil
freshly ground black pepper

*

For the cheese

rind cheese such as époisses, livarot, munster, rotschmierkäse, camembert and brie are suitable. Many of these cheeses are sold in little baskets and can, once all the plastic has been removed, be heated directly in the basket. Alternatively, place the cheese in a small ovenproof dish.

EEL UNAGI

INGREDIENTS
Serves 4

2–3 mandarins
20 g (3/4 oz) frisée
50 g (1 3/4 oz) pumpernickel*
1 garlic clove
100 ml (3 1/2 fl oz) sweet soy sauce
2 tablespoons oil
4 × 60–80 g (2–2 3/4 oz) skinless smoked eel fillets
salt

*

Pumpernickel *is a rye bread made with sourdough, originally from the region of Westphalia in Germany. It's baked for at least 16 hours in a steam oven and as a result develops its typical taste: sweet, malty, caramel-flavoured, with a mild sourness.*

Unagi is the Japanese word for eel, which in Japan is enjoyed barbecued and basted with sweet soy sauce. From that harmonious combination, matched here with juicy-sweet mandarins and toasted tangy pumpernickel bread, comes one of the most surprising creations of the new craft-beer cuisine – a perfect match for many dark beers.

PREPARATION
25 minutes

METHOD

Peel the mandarins, removing any white pith. Cut the segments out of their dividing skins. Tear the frisée into small pieces, then wash and spin dry. Finely crumble the pumpernickel. Peel and very finely dice the garlic, then mix into the soy sauce.

Heat the oil in a frying pan then fry the eel fillets for 1–2 minutes on each side. Pour in the soy sauce mixture and boil for 1–2 minutes until thick. In a second frying pan, toast the pumpernickel crumbs without oil for 2 minutes, then season with salt.

Sit the eel on prewarmed plates, then drizzle over any sauce remaining in the pan. Decorate with the mandarin segments and frisée, scatter over the toasted pumpernickel and serve.

BEER STYLES: Dark, malty beers such as dark beer, rauchmärzen (smoked märzen) or porter.

SPECIAL RECOMMENDATION: IPA by AleSmith, San Diego, USA. IPA-ish tropical fruits pair perfectly with the Japanese-style eel dish. Also, the bitterness of the hops is strong enough to counter the soy sauce and garlic.

Eel unagi

Mussels in beer with sautéed dill potatoes and an andalouse sauce

MUSSELS IN BEER WITH SAUTÉED DILL POTATOES AND AN ANDALOUSE SAUCE

The French-sounding mayonnaise sauce with the indication of Andalusian origin is a classic of Belgian cuisine, delicately flavoured with tomato paste, pepper and a hint of tarragon, slightly soured with vinegar. It goes wonderfully well with another classic of Belgian cuisine: mussels in beer!

INGREDIENTS
Serves 4–6

Andalouse sauce
80 g (2½ oz) mayonnaise
1 teaspoon tomato paste (concentrated purée)
large pinch of dried tarragon
large pinch of smoked or sweet paprika
2 fresh tarragon sprigs
splash of tarragon vinegar or white wine vinegar
salt
espelette pepper

Dill potatoes
800 g (1 lb 12 oz) small to medium new potatoes, boiled until tender
60 ml (2 fl oz/¼ cup) olive oil
salt
freshly ground black pepper
freshly ground white pepper
1 bunch dill
20 g (¾ oz) butter

Mussels in beer
1.5 kg (3 lb 5 oz) blue mussels
20 g (¾ oz) fresh ginger
1 garlic clove
80 g (2¾ oz) leeks
50 g (1¾ oz) butter
1 bay leaf
100 ml (3½ fl oz) helles (pale) beer
salt

PREPARATION

35 minutes (plus cooking the potatoes the day before)

METHOD

For the andalouse sauce: Mix the mayonnaise with the tomato paste, dried tarragon and paprika until smooth. Finely chop the fresh tarragon and stir in. Season with vinegar, salt and espelette pepper. Set aside for at least 10 minutes for the flavours to infuse the mayonnaise. Stir once more.

For the dill potatoes: Peel the potatoes. Heat the oil in a frying pan and fry the potatoes for 6–8 minutes until golden brown. Season with salt and the peppers, and set aside in the pan. Then prepare the mussels. Shortly before the mussels are ready, put the potatoes on the heat again. Finely chop the dill and add to the potatoes with the butter. Stir through and serve with the mussels.

For the mussels in beer: Thoroughly scrub the mussels in cold water, then remove the hairy beards. Discard any mussels that no longer close when pushed. Peel and finely grate the ginger. Peel and finely dice the garlic. Slice the leeks in thin rings and wash thoroughly. Melt the butter in a large saucepan, add the garlic, ginger, bay leaf and leeks, then douse with the beer. Bring to the boil, season with salt and add the mussels. Cover and cook for 8 minutes. Serve hot with the sauce and potatoes.

BEER STYLES: Gueuze, lambic, gose.

SPECIAL RECOMMENDATION: Unfortunately very rare, but that makes it more rewarding: the gueuze by Cantillon in Brussels (see p. 119). More than 150 types of yeasts and bacteria ferment this beer and ensure, besides the typical sourness, highly complex flavours. Dark. Enigmatic.

BERLINER WEISSE WAS A BEER THREATENED WITH EXTINCTION.

BERLIN, GERMANY

BOGK-BIER PRIVATE BREWERY

THE ARCHAEOLOGIST

Andreas Bogk is a hacker, one of a breed of people who demonstrate two particular characteristics: the will to and the habit of getting to the bottom of things, as well as a skill for improvisation – perfect qualifications for a career as a craft-beer brewer.

'I was infected with the brewing virus in 2010 at a conference in Belgium – one of the greatest beer countries on the planet!' explains Andreas Bogk. The conference was actually about computer security, but in the evening program it offered, among other things, a three-hour brewing workshop. He took part, immediately found pleasure in this 'nerd sport' and has since applied himself intensively as a hobby brewer in his home kitchen.

After his first successes with different beer styles, and intensive study of their history and production techniques – as mentioned, hackers are used to getting to the bottom of things – he finally began to work on the beer style of the place he lives: Berliner weisse. Here he stumbled upon a sad history, because from the glory of former times for this regional specialty – in Berlin in 1850 there were more than 150 breweries producing weisse – there was at the time of his research only one left. And it didn't produce the beer in the traditional way either. Since 2005, weisse in Berlin had been made using a modern industrial process, and as a result lacked an extremely important component of the flavour profile compared to the old original: *Brettanomyces*, the very yeast type that's also responsible for the complex and deep flavours of Belgian lambic and gueuze.

What in the wine world is considered a clear flaw in a wine – producing a penetrating note of horse sweat or wet dog – in weisse and lambic is a necessary component for a rounded flavour spectrum. It's quite similar to the way that in many good perfumes musk, which on its own has an unpleasant stink, ensures the complexity and depth of the scent. The regional Berlin specialty with a verifiable documented history of more than 300 years was thus acutely threatened with extinction!

Bogk's ambition was awakened. His aim: to rescue weisse. How: through brewing it. Originally, of course, using the traditional procedure, with the same fermentation using lactic acid bacteria and

TO BREW BEER, IN PRINCIPLE ALL YOU NEED IS A POT AND A WAY TO MAKE A FIRE UNDER IT.

yeasts, and also using the authentic traditional top-fermenting yeasts. But where to get these specific yeasts and especially the *Brettanomyces*? At the only remaining brewery these strains had been out of use for years. An expert on Berliner weisse – professor of brewing techniques at the Technical University of Berlin – gave the decisive tip: classic Berliner weisse was bottled with cloudy yeast. It was possible, if not really probable, that the *Brettanomyces* in sealed bottles was still alive.

Bogk then went searching for old bottles containing original Berliner weisse – and struck gold. He bought a weisse on eBay made by VEB Getränkekombinat Berlin and dating from the 1980s. With the help of his girlfriend, who worked in a specially equipped laboratory, he actually managed to isolate and grow the original old *Brettanomyces* strains. Since then he's had a new 'pet' at home, which through loving 'occasional copying' (to quote Bogk) is saved from extinction.

The necessary basis for the preservation or reconstruction of the cultural icon that is Berliner weisse was thus located. What was still missing, though, in order to also share the cultural acquisition with others, was the founding of a regular brewery, including fulfilling its food and also tax requirements. To build a brewery without being able to provide the capital himself, Bogk started a crowd-funding campaign in the summer of 2012. He wanted to raise 3000 Euros in a month to buy materials – and was positively overrun with success. After about five hours the original target was reached. After a day the project was financed to the tune of 200 per cent, and after the funding deadline expired the sum had reached more than 21,000 Euros – more than 700 per cent of the original estimated amount! The extra money received was invested in larger and more professional equipment. After about two years of brewing activity, a specially rented cellar followed, in the Berlin suburb of Kreuzberg. But then came a surprising termination of the lease by the landlord and a brewing hiatus.

Meanwhile a few things happened. Other brewers arrived on the scene, who came upon the fruity, sour, low-alcohol and traditional, quite weakly hopped Berlin specialty. It was also picked up by the German slow-food movement and its 'Ark of Taste'. There was even a Berliner weisse summit. And the Privatbrauerei Bogk-Bier carries on. While at the same time a circle closed, in a way that could hardly have been more beautiful or rounder: because the space where the Privatbrauerei Bogk-Bier will brew in the future is on the site of the former Willner Brauerei in Berlin, which from 1949 to 1990 had been a department of VEB Getränkekombinat Berlin. Exactly the place where that weisse bottle was brewed, from which the rescued yeast cultures were isolated. The *Brettanomyces* are returning to their original workplace!

MELZER HALLE A.

BOGK BIER
Berliner Weiße
18 Monate
0,1L
gelagert!

TRAGKRAFT
395 Kp/m^2

Berliner Weiße
Bogk-Bier
Privatbrauerei

Schankbier
Berliner
Weisse

BERLINER
GROTER JAN
WEISSE
SCHANKBIER

NAPOLEON PRAISED BERLINER WEISSE AS THE CHAMPAGNE OF THE NORTH.

SCALLOPS FRIED IN BROWN BUTTER WITH A NECTARINE AND FRISÉE SALAD

The nutty brown butter underscores the unique taste of the scallops. The fruity mixture of ripe nectarine and bitter lettuce suits it perfectly. The subtle sourness of the vinaigrette comes from fresh gueuze beer.

INGREDIENTS

Serves 4

60 g (2 oz) frisée
3 tablespoons gueuze beer, or a fresh, sour, pale beer
1 teaspoon honey
3 tablespoons olive oil
1 tarragon sprig
salt
2 ripe nectarines
50 g (1¾ oz) butter
8–12 scallops

PREPARATION

20 minutes

METHOD

Tear the frisée into bite-sized pieces, then wash and spin dry. Make a vinaigrette by stirring together the beer, honey and olive oil. Finely chop the tarragon and stir in. Season with salt. Remove the stones from the nectarines, slice thinly and mix into the vinaigrette.

For the brown butter, melt the butter in a saucepan until bubbling and cook, stirring, until it turns a pale brown. Strain into a frying pan through a sieve lined with muslin (cheesecloth).

Heat the butter in the pan, add the scallops and fry for 2 minutes. Season with salt, turn over and fry for a further 2–3 minutes. Mix the frisée into the nectarine salad and divide between serving plates. Sit the scallops on top and drizzle with the remaining butter in the pan. Serve immediately.

BEER STYLES: Berliner weisse or other mildly sour wheat beers, gueuze.

SPECIAL RECOMMENDATION: Kampot White by Freigeist Bierkultur in Germany (see page 175), a white beer brewed with white pepper from Cambodia, with a subtle peppery heat that catapults this dish to the fine-dining level.

Scallops fried in brown butter with a nectarine and frisée salad

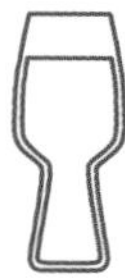

FISH 'N MUSHY PEAS

INGREDIENTS
Serves 4

Mushy peas
300 g (10½ oz) roasting potatoes
salt
400 g (14 oz/2⅔ cups) frozen peas
50 g (1¾ oz) butter
1 teaspoon finely grated organic lemon zest
a few splashes of lemon juice

Fish in beer batter
1 egg
100 ml (3½ fl oz) beer
100 g (3½ fl oz/⅔ cup) plain (all-purpose) flour, plus 2 tablespoons extra for dusting fish
salt
oil, for deep-frying
500 g (1 lb 2 oz) firm white fish fillets (e.g. pollock, haddock, whiting, catfish, Atlantic cod, rockling)
sea salt flakes

Fish 'n chips is considered the British national dish. In the pub version, fish 'n mushy peas, the fish is fried in beer batter and accompanied by a nourishing pea purée and dark beer – an outstanding idea!

PREPARATION
40 minutes

METHOD

For the mushy peas: Peel the potatoes, cut into rough pieces and boil in salted water until soft. Add the peas for 2 minutes. Drain and transfer to a saucepan with the butter. Let the butter melt. Season with salt, and the lemon zest and juice. Using a sturdy whisk, mash to a very rough paste.

Very gently and quickly use the point of a knife to purée the peas (this gives a lovely green colour – if you mash for too long and too thoroughly, though, it will be gluey). Keep warm.

For the fish in beer batter: Beat the egg with 2 tablespoons water and the beer. Add the sifted flour and mix to a smooth batter using an electric mixer. Season with salt and set aside for 10 minutes. Heat the oil in a deep-fryer to 190°C (370°F) (or heat about 500 ml/17 fl oz/ 2 cups oil in a tall narrow saucepan).

Cut the fish into pieces and toss it in the extra flour. Tap to remove any excess flour and dredge through the batter. Working in batches, fry the fish in the hot oil for 3–4 minutes until golden brown. Leave on paper towel to drain, sprinkle with sea salt flakes and serve with the mushy peas.

BEER STYLES: Stout, porter, black beer.

SPECIAL RECOMMENDATION: London Porter by Fuller's, England. A traditional English brew for an traditional English dish, and one of the best of this style worldwide.

Fish 'n mushy peas

YEAST-FLAVOURED

WHEAT BEER

As a craft beer almost exclusively found as hefeweizen (yeast wheat beer), but it is also good when atypically strongly hopped. Refreshingly fruity, besides citrus it can also have banana or clove notes. The stronger yeast clouding is pleasantly creamy on the palate.

ORIGIN	Bavaria, Germany
CHARACTER	Tangily fresh, lightly creamy
FERMENTATION	Top-fermented
ALCOHOL CONTENT	4.5–6% Vol.
DRINKING TEMP	7–11°C (45–52°F)
BEST GLASS	Wheat-beer glass
EXAMPLES	Schneider Weisse's Tap 7: Unser Original, Unertl's Gourmet Weisse, Hanscraft & Co.'s Bayerisch Nizza
RECIPES	The Whole Beast Rabbit (p. 152), Coppa Crispbreads (p. 29), Fried Baby Leeks (p. 87)
VARIANTS	Kristallweizen, weizenbock and doppelbock; Belgian witbier

Salt-baked sea bream with a lemon sabayon

SALT-BAKED SEA BREAM WITH A LEMON SABAYON

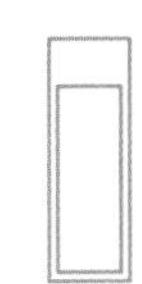

*Under the thyme and beer salt crust all the flavours of the sea bream are preserved – releasing its aroma when the salt crust is broken open at the table! A foamy lemon sabayon makes a very refined accompaniment.**

PREPARATION

30 minutes (plus 40 minutes baking)

METHOD

For the salt-baked sea bream: Preheat the oven to 220°C (430°F). Rinse the fish under cold water. Slice the lemon. Fill the stomach cavity of the bream with lemon slices and the bay leaves.

Finely chop the thyme. Beat the egg white to soft peaks and mix with the beer, thyme and sea salt.

Line a baking tray with baking paper and spread about one-third of the salt mixture over it to the size of fish. Lay the bream on top and cover with the remaining salt mixture. Press gently to ensure there are no holes or tears in the crust. Bake for 35 minutes.

For the lemon sabayon: In a stainless-steel bowl, mix together the beer, lemon zest and juice, sugar and salt until smooth.

Bring a hand's width of water to the boil in a saucepan, then reduce the heat and bring to a gentle simmer. Place the bowl on top and beat the sabayon, preferably with an electric mixer, for a few minutes until creamy and foamy. Add the butter at the end and stir until melted. Add more salt and sugar if needed, and season with a hint of cayenne pepper.

To finish: Remove the fish from the oven, break the salt crust on one side and remove. Peel off the fish skin and lift out the fillets using a fork and spoon. Transfer to prewarmed plates. Pour over the sabayon. Then lift off the skeleton, take out the fillets, remove the skin and enjoy a second helping.

BEER STYLES: Pale beers in which the bitterness isn't too dominant, wheat beer, kölsch.

SPECIAL RECOMMENDATION: Forbidden Planet by Bluejacket, Washington DC, USA. A dry-hopped kölsch with the intense aroma of tropical fruit. Light enough to not dominate the fish, interesting enough to add complexity to the dish.

INGREDIENTS

Serves 2

Salt-baked sea bream

1 large (450–550 g/1 lb – 1 lb 3 oz) sea bream, gutted and cleaned

1 organic lemon

2 bay leaves

4 thyme sprigs or ½ teaspoon dried thyme

1 egg white

2 tablespoons beer

1 kg (2 lb 3 oz) coarse sea salt

Lemon sabayon

2 egg yolks

100 ml (3½ fl oz) pale beer

1 teaspoon grated organic lemon zest

splash of lemon juice

pinch of sugar

pinch of salt

20 g (¾ oz) cold butter, diced

cayenne pepper

*

Sabayon
is the French word for the foamy sauce beaten over a boiling water bath, which can be sweet and hearty. It's largely based on egg yolk and wine or a spirit. Sabayon is related to the Italian zabaglione, a sweet wine-foam cream made with marsala.

SMOKED HERRING FROM THE OVEN

INGREDIENTS
Serves 4

Rissolée potatoes
600 g (1 lb 5 oz) boiling potatoes
60 ml (2 fl oz/¼ cup) oil
salt

Beer beurre blanc
2 French shallots
1 tablespoon olive oil
1 bay leaf
1 teaspoon mustard seeds
1 heaped teaspoons sugar
250 ml (8½ fl oz/1 cup) beer, plus an extra splash to finish
150 g (5½ oz) cold butter, diced
salt
a little lemon juice

Spinach and herrings
4 small smoked herrings
600 g (1 lb 5 oz) English spinach leaves
2 French shallots
20 g (¾ oz) butter
salt
freshly ground black pepper

Rissolée potatoes are the princess version of fried potatoes, small and delicate and crisp. Perfect with a foamy beer beurre blanc sauce, peppery spinach and warm smoked fish straight from the oven.

PREPARATION
40 minutes

METHOD

For the rissolée potatoes: Peel and finely dice the potatoes. Heat the oil over medium heat in a large non-stick frying pan and fry the potatoes for 20–25 minutes, shaking the pan frequently. Season with salt.

For the beer beurre blanc: Peel and finely dice the shallots. Heat the oil in a saucepan and sauté the shallots until transparent. Add the bay leaf and mustard seeds, and stir through the sugar. Cook for 1 minute. Pour in the beer and boil vigorously, uncovered, for 8–10 minutes.

Strain the sauce through a sieve into a second saucepan and bring to the boil. Remove from the heat and gradually add the cold butter pieces and mix in with the tip of the knife. Season the thick sauce with salt, lemon juice and an extra splash of beer. Keep warm.

For the spinach and herrings: Warm the herrings for about 10 minutes in an 80°C (180°F) oven. Wash the spinach and spin dry. Finely dice the shallots and sauté in the butter in a frying pan until transparent. Add the spinach, cook until wilted, and season with salt and pepper.

Divide the herrings and potatoes between prewarmed plates. Reheat (without boiling) the sauce and make it foamy with a hand-held blender. Drizzle over the dish and serve.

BEER STYLES: Sour beers like weisse, gose, lambic or gueuze.

SPECIAL RECOMMENDATION: Miami Madness by J. Wakefield Brewing, Miami, USA. A top-rated weisse with decent sourness and a basket full of fruit flavour – which perfectly suits both the fish and beurre blanc.

Smoked herring from the oven

AND THEN WE JUST SAID, 'LET'S MAKE A BEER TOGETHER.'

BERLIN, GERMANY

BRLO

THE START-UP BREWERY

Presumably the most frequently asked question for the young brewery start-up in the German capital must be about the pronunciation and meaning of the at-first cryptic name. Please, we'll gladly help you with that: BRLO is pronounced something like 'Bearr-low' and is the original Old Slavic name for Berlin.

What happens when two young design, sales and marketing experts with the intention of doing 'something with beer' at some point meet a passionate brewer who had his first hands-on experience at the age of 16, followed by training and finally a brewing diploma? Quite simple: there arises one of the hippest brands the German craft-beer scene has yet offered!

On 1 November 2014 the first beer appeared on the market from BRLO, a start-up from two business managers Katharina Kurz and Christian Laase and master brewer Michael Lembke. Kurz and Laase knew each other from studying together at the European Business School. Lembke studied at the renowned brewing research and teaching institution Versuchs- und Lehranstalt für Brauerei (VLB), in Berlin, where these days he still works one day a week as a research assistant. Together they worked towards tearing the idea of craft beer away from its specialist niche existence and providing beers far beyond factory-made monotony to a young inner-city clientele.

The appearance of BRLO on the scene is exactly what you'd expect from a start-up in the German capital: accentuating youth and city life. A successful label design, from the Hamburg agency Lutz Hermann Design, which has otherwise worked in the perfume and cosmetics sector, is part of that, as is a stylish modern website. Their publicity materials include drinking recommendations, which beside food pairings also include beers 'for snogging' or 'for skinny-dipping'. Until now it was rare to find so much youthful urbanity in the craft-beer scene.

The brewing portfolio comprises three different styles: a helles, a pale ale and a porter, all of them brilliant examples of their kind. For the Berlin Beer Week 2015 the range was augmented to include a weisse. Originally it was only considered a test brew, but thanks to its success, the BRLO team have been thinking about making the old traditional Berlin style a permanent part of their brewing program. For a brewery whose logo, besides a head of grain and a hop cone, also carries a small Berlin bear, this is actually almost an urgent consideration.

You won't find BRLO going after the bitterness records sought by other craft-beer

IN THE MEDIUM TERM, HAVING OUR OWN BREWERY IS A CONSIDERATION – IF ONLY TO GIVE OUR BEERS A HOME.

brewers – extreme hop excesses appeal to master brewer Michael Lembke very little. Other things interest him. For example, the yeasts used. He raised them himself in Berlin – there's got to be a lot of professional brewing honour in that. The frightening intensity of IPAs occasionally experienced by novices at their first contact doesn't happen with BRLO ales. Nevertheless, with its four American and one German hop cultivar, it demonstrates the typical fruity notes of its aromatic hops.

With the recently brewed weisse, too, you sense BRLO's extremely conscious brewing philosophy of paring back. In conversation Lembke makes clear his great admiration for Jean Marie Rock, the master brewer for many years with the Belgian Trappist beer maker Orval, who is legendary for using *Brettanomyces* in his beers. However, with his own weisse he passed on the opportunity of using these special yeasts, which would have lent the beer an unusual darkness and occasional unsettlingly cryptic flavours. A weisse brewed directly with woodruff was something that interested him much more. But as long as BRLO doesn't have a brewery of its own at its disposal, we should expect such experiments.

Because at the moment BRLO still brews all its beers as a gypsy brewer in two medium-sized breweries in eastern Germany – naturally, the three founders take this seriously, under the personal supervision of master brewer Lembke. The bottom-fermented helles, along with the photos opposite, is made in the Klosterbrauerei Neuzelle, which dates back to 1589; the top-fermented porter and pale ales in the Brauerei Landsberg in Saxony-Anhalt, which is equally rich in tradition. They use their own recipes developed in Berlin and with raw materials purchased themselves for BRLO, it's important to note. 'Designed in Berlin. Assembled in Landsberg [or Neuzelle],' it says on the label. You can read about the origins and types of the hops used, and the organic certification of the malts, on their home page, as well as which breweries are hosting their beers.

In the medium term the three young founders are planning to build their own brewery in Berlin – naturally with a bar attached: 'If only to give our beers a home!' says Katharina Kurz. For the bulk brews they will still very probably also fall back on other breweries. Within the craft-beer scene elsewhere it's also common practice. And what's more, for many middle-sized established breweries it's a very welcome improvement in capacity utilisation in the daily struggle for commercial survival. A classic win-win situation – the 'sharing economy of beer brewing', as Katharina Kurz calls it, in practice.

In that way BRLO is every bit the young, exuberant, capital-city start-up. Just as it is with its remarkable approach to social engagement and sustainability. A fixed amount from the proceeds from each bottle sold goes towards social and cultural projects in the capital city. It supports the Kulturloge Berlin, an organisation devoted to making the arts accessible to everyone, and recently sponsored a number of beehives. There's one thing for certain: there are worse ways to do 'something with beer'...

Nr. 807
SECKMÜHLE
Mühlenbauanstalt und Maschinenfabrik vorm.
GEBRÜDER SECK, DRESDEN

BRŁO

BRŁO

BRŁO
CRAFT BEER
PALE ALE

PALE ALE
NEW
NEW

en

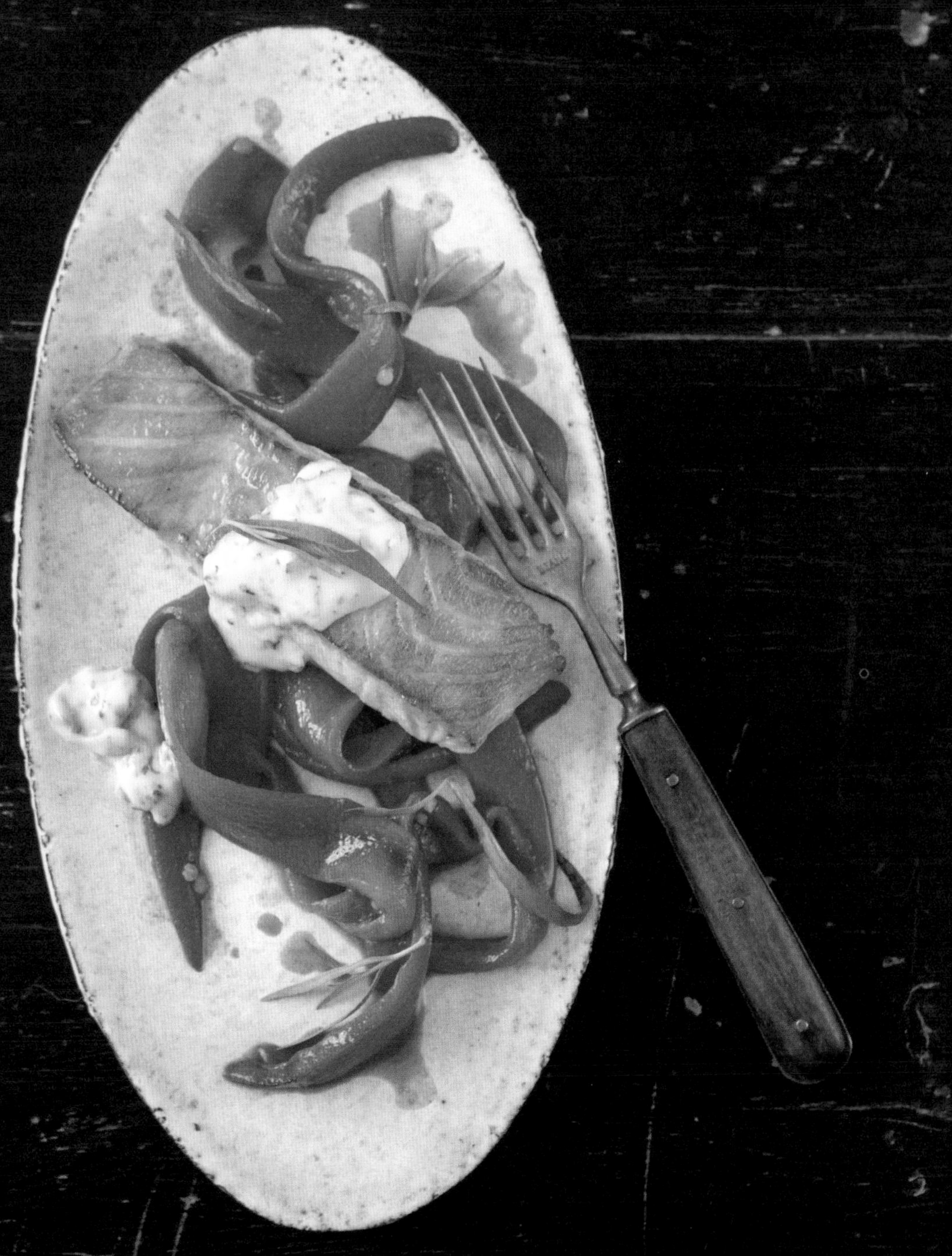

Pan-fried salmon on capsicum with tarragon mayonnaise

PAN-FRIED SALMON ON CAPSICUM WITH TARRAGON MAYONNAISE

A refined fish dish, aromatic with herbs, which goes well with a quaffable India pale ale. Very well even!

PREPARATION

25 minutes

METHOD

For the fried capsicum: Peel the capsicums with a vegetable peeler, then halve them lengthways and remove the seeds and stalk. Cut into wide strips, sprinkle with salt and fry in hot oil over medium heat for 8–10 minutes or until soft. Season them with paprika, sugar and cayenne pepper. Add the stock and boil, uncovered, for 1–2 minutes. Keep warm.

For the tarragon mayonnaise: Make a sauce by mixing together the mayonnaise and sour cream. Chop two of the fresh tarragon sprigs finely and stir them along in with the dried tarragon. Season with salt, sugar and a splash of tarragon vinegar.

For the pan-fried salmon: Season the salmon fillets with salt. Heat the oil and butter together in a frying pan over medium heat and fry the fillets for 2–3 minutes on each side, or to your taste.

Lay the fish on the capsicum, scatter over the picked leaves from the remaining tarragon sprig and serve with the sauce.

TIP: This dish goes well with baguettes.

BEER STYLES: Pale and red ales, IPA, session IPA.

SPECIAL RECOMMENDATION: Ponto Sessionable India Pale Ale by Pizza Port, California, USA. This slightly lighter session IPA doesn't over dominate the aroma of the dish

INGREDIENTS

Serves 4

Fried capsicum

500 g (1 lb 12 oz) red capsicums (bell peppers), preferably long
salt
60 ml (2 fl oz/¼ cup) olive oil
1 teaspoon sweet paprika
pinch of sugar
cayenne pepper, to taste
100 ml (3½ fl oz) vegetable stock

Tarragon mayonnaise

60 g (2 oz) mayonnaise
60 g (2 oz/¼ cup) sour cream
3 fresh tarragon sprigs
large pinch of dried tarragon
salt
pinch of sugar
splash of tarragon vinegar or white wine vinegar

Pan-fried salmon

4 × 160 g (5½ oz) salmon fillet slices
salt
2 tablespoons olive oil
20 g (¾ oz) butter

BEER-BRAISED PORK BELLY WITH BLUEBERRIES AND RED COLESLAW

INGREDIENTS
Serves 4–6

Beer-braised pork
1 kg (2 lb 3 oz) boneless pork belly with rind
salt
1 tablespoon lard
2 onions
2 tablespoons soft brown sugar
500 ml (17 fl oz/2 cups) beer
250 ml (8½ fl oz/1 cup) beef stock
150 g (5½ oz) blueberries
salt
freshly ground black pepper

Red coleslaw
300 g (10½ oz) red cabbage
salt
2 tablespoons balsamic vinegar
1 tablespoon honey
1 tablespoon walnut oil or other nut oil
3 tablespoons olive oil

A beer belly is a beautiful thing! This roast, which comes out of the oven as soft as butter and with a crispy crust, is cooked in a tasty beer broth with sweet blueberries and accompanied by fresh red coleslaw.

PREPARATION

25 minutes (plus 2 hours to cook)

METHOD

For the beer-braised pork: Score the pork rind in a lattice down to the meat. Season the belly with salt. Melt the lard in a flameproof roasting tin on the stove top. Lay the belly in the tin with the rind facing down. Fry the rind until light brown (it can spit a little, so it's best to use a splatter guard).

Preheat the oven to 175°C (350°F). Halve the onions, then peel them and cut into wedges. Still on the stove top, turn the pork over, add the onions, and sauté until transparent. Add the sugar and allow to caramelise slightly. Pour in the beer and bring to the boil.

Transfer to the oven and cook for 60 minutes. Pour in the stock and return to the oven for another 60 minutes. Add the blueberries 5 minutes before the end of cooking. Season the jus with salt and pepper.

For the red coleslaw: Thinly slice or finely grate the cabbage. Season with salt and knead in the balsamic vinegar, honey, walnut oil and olive oil until soft.

TIPS: If you like you can skim the fat off the tasty braising liquid before you add the blueberries using a fat separator jug. Or thicken it a little with some cornflour (cornstarch).

Cook a few potatoes with the pork belly, then mash them!

BEER STYLES: Not too dark, malt-flavoured, weakly hopped beers, such as red ale or a pale bock. Alternatively, try a gueuze, with a distinctive sourness that makes the fat in the pork easier to digest.

SPECIAL RECOMMENDATION: The gueuze Mariage Parfait by Boon, Belgium – in fact, a successful marriage between the braised pork and something completely different: strong sourness with marked aromatic complexity and depth. For advanced students of craft beer.

Beer-braised pork belly with blueberries and red coleslaw

BRUSSELS MUSEUM VAN DE

SOLD OUT
SOLD OUT

GUEUZE & KRIEK
DE LA MAISON
CANTILLON
RUE GHEUDE, 56-58

37
R

BRUSSELS, BELGIUM

BRASSERIE CANTILLON

THE TIME MACHINE

'Brussels Gueuze Museum' – the shining plaque on the wooden door already indicates that this is a place steeped in history. Cantillon beer has been brewed in this family business since 1900 – in the world's original beer style.

Before us sits a heavy wide decanter, of the kind once only used for the best wines. In it, a luminous deep gold, is a beer – Zwanze 2012 – a fruit lambic fermented with regional rhubarb. 'This is probably the best beer that I've ever brewed in my life!' master brewer Jean van Roy says with pride when we try it. And indeed, what we taste is stunning. Complex, almost unfathomably deep, with a clear rhubarb fruitiness and over it all a strong, refreshing sourness. And to top it off: with every minute in the decanter and glass the beer becomes better and more complex.

Lambic and gueuze have been produced in the family business Cantillon since 1900. Traditional Belgian sour beers, brewed using a method that hasn't changed much in more than 8000 years, when people with grain farms and grain processing also developed the art of brewing beer. Modern beer drinkers, who are no longer used to sour beers – although throughout most of the history of beer, all beers have tasted sour – flinch when it comes to sourness in beer, which is a mistake. Because 'Lambic is the perfect beer to cook with. It has very little bitterness and lots of refreshing sourness,' says Jean. 'Thirty to 40 years ago cooking with beer, especially with lambic, was still widespread here!'

In subsequent years, apparently, that unfortunately changed. Twenty to 25 years ago Cantillon's existence was also acutely threatened by the raging course of brewery death. In 1978, Jean's father, Jean-Pierre, finally had the idea that saved them. He opened the brewery to visitors and turned it, with its old traditional production methods and machines, some of which date from the nineteenth century, into the Brussels Gueuze Museum. What back then elicited bitter resistance from Jean's grandfather ('You don't let strangers into your brewery!'), subsequently proved the saviour of the business. Today about 40,000 people visit the brewery each year.

Lambic is traditionally fermented spontaneously, without any active addition of yeast cultures and only through infection from wild yeasts in the air. At Cantillon this infection – 'the magic' – as Jean puts it, not

YOU HAVE TO DO THINGS WITH LOVE, BECAUSE IN THE END PEOPLE FIND THIS LOVE AGAIN IN THE GLASS.

without an undertone of respect, happens in what's called a coolship, a large basin under the roof in which the boiled wort is cooled overnight. About 100 different yeast strains and many more than 50 different bacterial cultures settle here in the rafters. Almost all lead the beers made here through fermentation to their complex aromatics.

The fermentation and maturation of the beers then follows, for a period of one to three years, in used wooden barrels of 200–500 litres (50–130 gallons). Storing them demands an enormous amount of room – to produce 100 litres (26 gallons) of lambic or gueuze, Cantillon needs more than 1 square metre (10 square feet). The available surface area at the moment only allows production of about 170,000 litres (45,000 gallons) per year. Another warehouse very nearby should soon allow increased capacity.

To stabilise the beer for its long maturation time, it's hopped with six times the normal amount used in brewing. Nevertheless, it's not too bitter. The hops that are added have been stored for about three years, during which time a large proportion of the alpha acid responsible for their bitterness can break down. After about a year the lambic – by this time practically free of carbonic acid – is ready to be worked upon further. Through the addition of fruit and supplementary secondary fermention, it becomes, for example, kriek (with sour cherries) or fruit lambic (with raspberries or other fruits). At Cantillon whole fruits are put in – no purées or even concentrates. About 200–300 grams per litre (28–42 oz per gallon) are added to each barrel. And then finally it goes into bottles to ferment further. For this reason, traditional bottle-fermented fruit lambic (look for 'oude' [old] on the label), in contrast to modern factory-made variants, is also bone dry – almost all the sugar that was in the beer has been fermented by different yeasts.

A part of the lambic matures further and finally becomes gueuze – a cuvée of, as a rule, five or six different lambic barrels with an age of one to three years that then ferments further in the bottle and thus forms its fine, almost Champagne-like bubbles, which beside its sourness and complex aromatics marks an 'oude' gueuze.

WE BREW IN THE WORLD'S ORIGINAL BREWING STYLE.

We most warmly recommend every visitor to Brussels to visit the time machine called Cantillon. To allow yourself to be carried for a short time to another century, to see, to feel the dedication with which beer is brewed here. And naturally, to take with you a few of the top-quality beers brewed here to try: for example the Rosé de Gambrinus, fermented with raspberries; or the fruity and intensely peppery Pineau d'Aunis, fermented with grape must from the Loire.

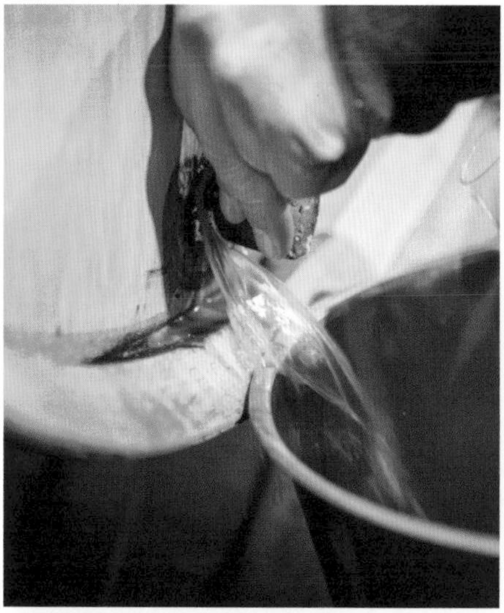

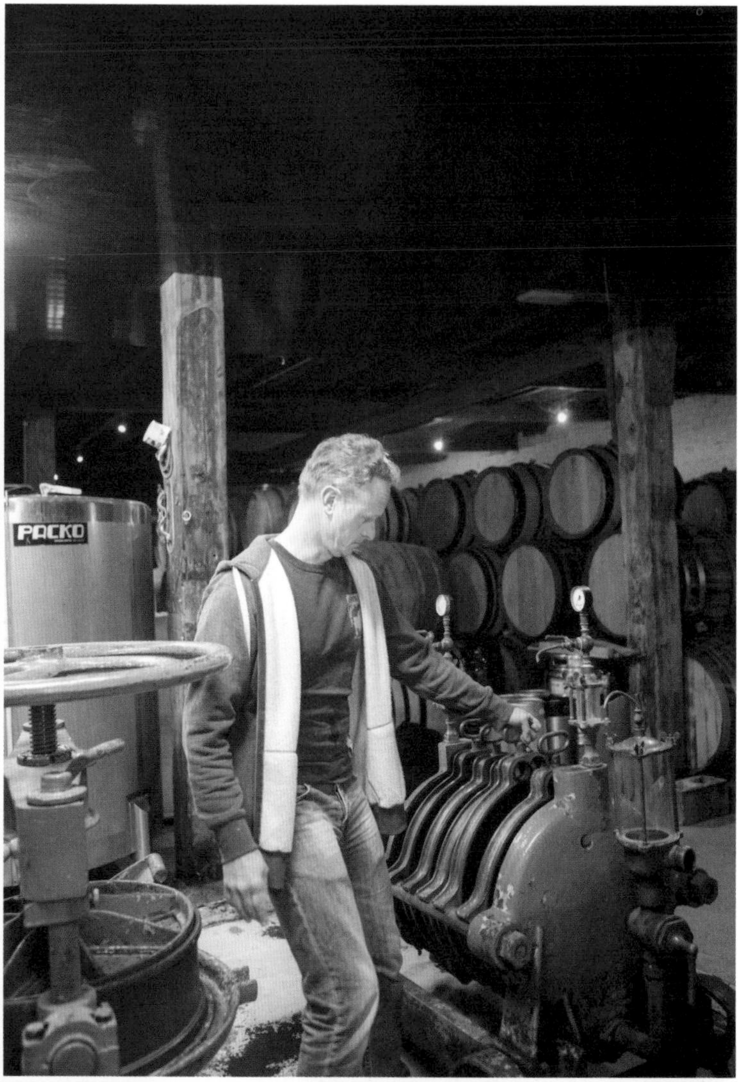
PACKO

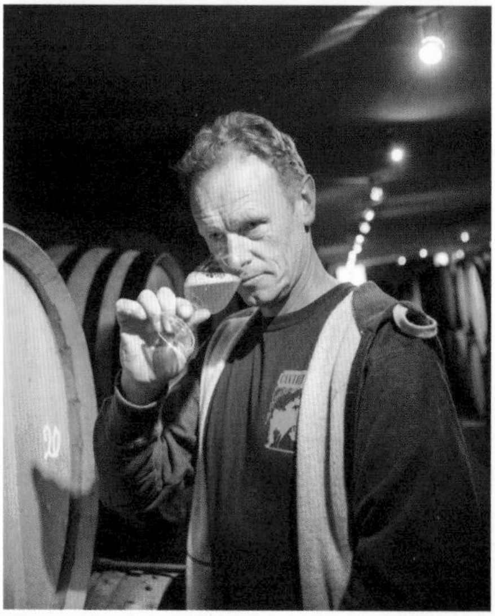

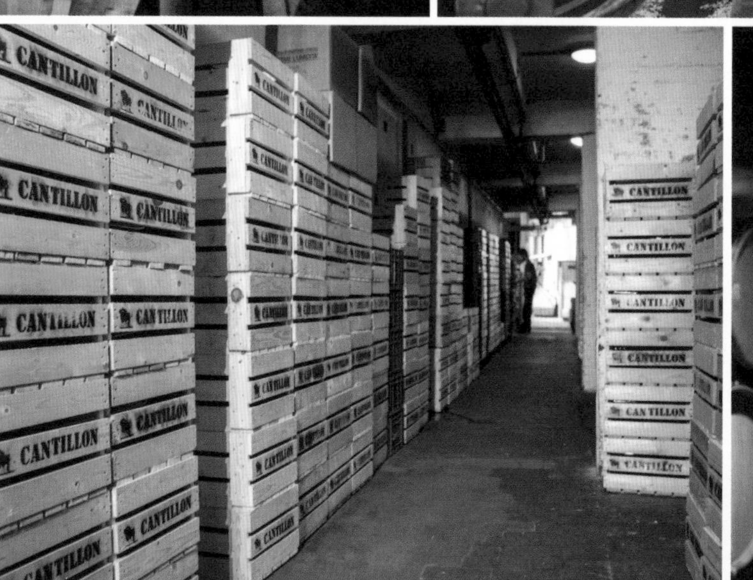

CANTILLON

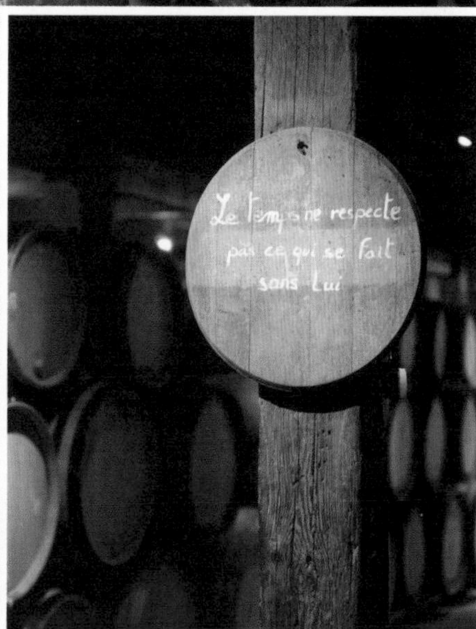

Le temps ne respecte
pas ce qui se fait
sans Lui

LAMBIC IS THE MISSING LINK BETWEEN WINE, BEER AND CIDER.

DOUBLE VEAL CUTLET ON OVEN CARROTS WITH VANILLA BUTTER

INGREDIENTS
Serves 2

Oven carrots
600 g (1 lb 5 oz) multicoloured baby carrots
75 ml (2½ fl oz) olive oil
1 garlic clove
½ teaspoon fennel seeds
1 tablespoon honey
salt
freshly ground black pepper
200 ml (7 fl oz) dark beer

Cutlet with vanilla butter
1 double veal cutlet (about 500 g/1 lb 2 oz)
2 tablespoons olive oil
salt
freshly ground black pepper
½ vanilla bean
20 g (¾ oz) softened butter
1 tablespoon pine nuts
2 chervil sprigs

This cutlet for two with braised carrots straight from the oven is butter-soft and served with vanilla butter, which combines the aromas of the sweet carrots and the tasty meat perfectly. Pine nuts provide crunch and the nutty notes. A new favourite recipe.

PREPARATION
40 minutes

METHOD

For the oven carrots: Preheat the oven to 220 °C (430 °F). Thoroughly wash the unpeeled carrots under hot water, then halve them lengthways. Heat the oil in a flameproof roasting tin over medium heat on the stove top, then fry the carrots for 8 minutes. Peel and dice the garlic, and stir in with the fennel seeds and honey. Season with salt and pepper. Pour in the beer, bring to the boil, then transfer to the oven and cook the carrots for 15 minutes.

For the cutlet with vanilla butter: Score the fat along the double cutlet in a lattice. Lay the cutlet, fat side down, in an ovenproof frying pan with the oil and brown the fat.

Turn the oven down to 200 °C (400 °F). Fry the meat in the pan on all sides for 5 minutes, then season with salt and pepper. Slide the pan into the oven and cook for a further 6 minutes on each side.

Halve the vanilla bean, and scrape the seeds. Stir the seeds into the softened butter with a pinch of salt. Toast the pine nuts in a dry frying pan. Remove the meat and carrots from the oven, top with the vanilla butter, scatter over the pine nuts and the roughly picked chervil leaves, and serve.

BEER STYLES: Dark toasty beers such as porter, stout or imperial stout. Especially good are its barrel-matured varieties, often with hints of vanilla.

SPECIAL RECOMMENDATION: Cocoa Psycho by BrewDog from Scotland, a heavy imperial stout with – besides strong coffee and cocoa flavours – intense vanilla notes.

Double veal cutlet on oven carrots with vanilla butter

Chicken ragout in a dark beer sauce with crisp chicken skin

CHICKEN RAGOUT IN A DARK BEER SAUCE WITH CRISP CHICKEN SKIN

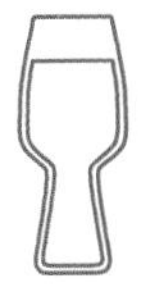

Only the tender leg meat is used in this dark beer chicken stew with mushrooms, while the chicken skin crisps in the oven to crunchy–soft. At the finale it's joined by brussels sprouts straight from the pan and toasted rolled oats.This is how elegant beer cuisine can be.

PREPARATION

40 minutes

INGREDIENTS

Serves 4

4 free-range boneless chicken thighs (order from your butcher)
salt
75 ml (2½ fl oz) oil
4 French shallots
1 garlic clove
pepper
1 teaspoon sugar
1 tablespoon sweet paprika
1–2 teaspoons dried summer savoury
100 ml (3½ fl oz) beer
500 ml (17 fl oz/2 cups) chicken stock
200 g (7 oz) button mushrooms
2 tablespoons traditional rolled (porridge) oats
8 brussels sprouts

METHOD

Preheat the oven to 200 °C (400 °F). Remove the skin from the chicken and spread it in a roasting tin lined with baking paper. Season lightly with salt. Lay a second sheet of baking paper on top and weigh it down with a second tin or a baking tray. Bake high up in the oven until crispy.

Cut the chicken into two pieces. Heat about 60 ml (2 fl oz/¼ cup) of the oil in a deep frying pan then sear the chicken until brown all over.

Peel and finely dice the shallots and garlic, then add to the pan and fry for 2 minutes. Season with salt, pepper and sugar. Add the paprika and summer savoury, and fry briefly. Add the beer and bring to the boil. Pour in the stock and cook, uncovered, for 15–20 minutes until thick.

Clean the mushrooms and cook in a large dry frying pan (cooked without oil this way, the mushrooms will develop a slightly smoky, toasted note). Season with salt and set aside. Toast the rolled oats in a dry frying pan until light brown, then season lightly with salt.

Cut the stalks off the brussels sprouts high enough to release the leaves.Separate into single leaves, then chop the pale central core. Heat the remaining oil in a frying pan over medium heat, add the brussels sprouts, season with salt and stir for 2 minutes. Keep warm.

Remove the chicken skin from the oven, drain on paper towel and break into pieces. Add the mushrooms to the ragout, bring to the boil, and season with salt and pepper. Arrange the stew on warmed plates, with the chicken skin, brussels sprouts and rolled oats, and serve immediately.

BEER STYLES: Stout, dark beer, porter.

SPECIAL RECOMMENDATION: Imperial Stout by Samuel Smith, England – a match made in heaven.

STRONGLY HOPPED

PILSNER

The most widespread beer style in the world. It's bottom-fermented in cold conditions and became more popular once mechanical cooling was widely available. Refreshingly crisp in character. Because of the mass of soulless factory beers it's often wrongly underestimated.

ORIGIN	Pilsen, Czech Republic
CHARACTER	Fresh, crisp, hop-flavoured
FERMENTATION	Top-fermented
ALCOHOL CONTENT	4.5–6% Vol.
DRINKING TEMP	6–9°C (43–48°F)
BEST GLASS	Beer tulip
EXAMPLES	Schönramer's Pilsner, Schönramer's Grünhopfen Pils, Pilsner Urquell, Brauprojekt 777's Pilsss
RECIPES	Beer Pizza (p. 44), Fried Little Fish (p. 27), Fried Baby Leeks (p. 87), Calf Heart (p. 169), Veal Rissoles (p. 155), The Whole Beast Rabbit (p. 152)
VARIANTS	Bohemian pilsner (as a rule malty and fuller bodied)

Venison schnitzel with potato gremolata and beer sauce

VENISON SCHNITZEL WITH POTATO GREMOLATA AND BEER SAUCE

In tribute to the original wiener schnitzel, here's a modification with soft tasty venison in combination with an aromatic beer sauce and lemony potato and parsley gremolata.

INGREDIENTS
Serves 4

Beer sauce
400 g (14 oz) onions
2 tablespoons olive oil
1 small apple
1 tablespoon soft brown sugar
1 garlic clove
2 thyme sprigs
330 ml (11 fl oz) witbier
500 ml (17 fl oz/2 cups) beef stock
2 Kemm brown biscuits (cookies)*
40 g (1½ oz) cold butter, diced
salt

Venison schnitzel
400 g (14 oz) venison steaks
35 g (1¼ oz/¼ cup) plain (all-purpose) flour
1 large egg, lightly beaten
120 g (4½ oz) breadcrumbs
75 ml (2½ fl oz) oil
30 g (1 oz) butter
salt

Potato gremolata
150 g (5½ oz) potatoes, cooked the day before, peeled
2 tablespoons olive oil
½ bunch flat-leaf (Italian) parsley
1 teaspoon grated organic lemon zest
salt

PREPARATION
40 minutes

METHOD
For the beer sauce: Peel the onions and slice into strips. Heat the oil in a frying pan and fry the onion until golden brown. Peel and dice the apple. Add the sugar to the onion and stir until dissolved. Peel and finely dice the garlic, then stir it in with the diced apple and the thyme. Fry for 1 minute. Pour in the beer and boil, uncovered, for 5 minutes. Pour in the stock and boil for a further 5 minutes. Add the biscuits and stir until dissolved. Remove the thyme. Pour this sauce base into a high-sided container and purée with a hand-held blender. Gradually add the cold butter, blending until each piece is incorporated. Season the sauce with salt and keep warm in a saucepan.
For the venison schnitzel: Wash the venison, dab dry with paper towel, and cut into eight thin schnitzels. Coat in the flour, dredge through the beaten egg and toss in the breadcrumbs. Heat the oil in a large non-stick frying pan, then fry the schnitzels for 3–4 minutes on each side until golden brown. Add the butter, let it bubble and move the schnitzels around in the foaming butter for another minute. Drain the schnitzels on paper towel and season with salt. Keep warm in a 50°C (120°F) oven.
For the potato gremolata: Peel and dice the potatoes. Heat the oil in a non-stick frying pan and fry the potato until golden brown. Chop the parsley. Add the parsley and lemon zest to the light-brown potato pieces and season with salt. Divide the gremolata between the schnitzels and serve with the sauce.

BEER STYLES: For the sauce, preferably witbier or gose; as an accompaniment, a strongly hopped pilsner tastes good

SPECIAL RECOMMENDATION: Calabaza Blanca by Jolly Pumpkin Artisan Ales, Michigan, USA. A medium sour witbier brewed with coriander and orange peel, which gives the sauce depth and substance.

*

Kemm brown biscuits *have been made by the Hamburg bakery Kemm since 1782. Substitute plain gingerbread or ginger biscuits (cookies).*

CREAMY MALT BEER POLENTA WITH SAUSAGE AND A FENNEL SALAD

INGREDIENTS
Serves 4

Fennel salad
½ teaspoon fennel seeds
juice of 1 orange
1–2 teaspoons white wine vinegar
2 tablespoons olive oil
250 g (9 oz) fennel with fronds
salt

Polenta with sausage
800 ml (27 fl oz) chicken stock
100 ml (3½ fl oz) malt beer
50 g (1¾ oz) butter
1 tablespoon olive oil
120 g (4½ oz) polenta
100 g (3½ oz) bergkäse cheese
salt
pepper
3 tablespoons oil
4–8 thick sausages

This hearty mountain meal from the Italian Alps goes perfectly with dark, malty beers. The creamy cheese polenta tastes best with thick sausages, while the fennel salad provides freshness and crunch.

PREPARATION
45 minutes

METHOD

For the fennel salad: Very finely grind the fennel seeds with a mortar and pestle, then mix with the orange juice, vinegar and oil to make a vinaigrette. Finely slice the fennel bulb with a mandoline or knife. Chop the fronds and toss everything with the vinaigrette. Season with salt.

For the polenta with sausage: Bring the chicken stock to the boil with the beer, butter and olive oil. Stir in the polenta with a whisk. Cook for 15 minutes over low heat, stirring frequently with a wooden spoon.

Grate the cheese and stir it into the polenta. Season with salt and pepper. Remove from the heat then cover and set aside until the sausages are ready.

Heat the 3 tablespoons of oil in a frying pan over medium heat and fry the sausages for 10–15 minutes.

Stir the polenta, then arrange it on warmed plates or in little serving pans with the sausages and fennel salad.

BEER STYLES: Less bitter, malt-flavoured beers such as classic Bavarian dark or malt beers.

SPECIAL RECOMMENDATION: Dunkel by Heater Allen Brewing, Oregon, USA. A Bavarian-style dark lager, mostly dominated by malty aromas, which makes it an almost perfect choice for a dish that originated in the Italian Alps region.

Creamy malt beer polenta with sausage and a fennel salad

Hopfen
und
Malz
Gott
erhalt's

KELHEIM, BAVARIA

SCHNEIDER WEISSE

DIVERSITY

On the edge of the largest continuous hop cultivation area in the world lies the council town Kelheim. Here of all places they brew a beer style for which, until a few years ago, the subject of hops was of secondary importance.

'The DNA of the business was already so well established that we're taking new risks!' reports the owner, Georg Schneider VI, who then explains, not without pride, that his great-great-great-grandfather acquired the brewing rights to weissbier from the Bavarian royal house at a time when this beer was anything but in vogue. 'Brown beer' brewed with bottom fermentation was then in demand, and production of top-fermented weissbiers had apparently stopped almost completely in the 'Königlich Weissen Hofbräuhaus' (royal court brewery). Georg Schneider I, however, was so convinced that weissbier had a future that he entered into negotiations with the Bavarian court brewery. At that time the right to brew weissbier – the so-called regal beer – still lay exclusively with the Bavarian royal house. This was an unavoidable consequence of the Purity Law of 1516, which only approved barley for brewing, not least to reserve nutritionally important wheat for bakers.

Thirty years later, brewing with wheat was legal again – although only as an exclusive privilege, granted in the event to bind a particular princely house to the royal court. When Georg Schneider I finally acquired the right from the Bavarian court, he was the first commoner in almost 500 years legally allowed to brew weissbier in Bavaria. Incidentally, there's a widespread misconception that weissbier is brewed exclusively from wheat malt; the malt mixture of a classic wheat beer is, however, up to 50 per cent barley malt.

But back to hops. As already noted, they actually play a subordinate role in the aroma profile of a weissbier. It's dominated by the fruit and herb aromas produced by the yeast during fermentation. Above all the main aromas of banana and cloves, whose skilful balance determines the quality of a really good weissbier. But when Schneider's master brewer, Hans-Peter Drexler, got to know the then still new world of American hops on a trip to the United States, he had an idea. The intense citrus aromas of Cascade hops had especially grabbed Drexler's attention. At the time it was still widespread practice to serve kristallweizen with a lemon slice – aromatically a completely sensible addition, but considered by many brewers to be a bad habit that overwhelms the delicate beer aromas. Why not use hops to integrate the completely harmonising aromas of citrus? The consequence of this thought was the Wiesen Edel-weisse, brewed to this receipe for the first time in 2000. A wheat beer with fresh dry notes, among other things hopped with American Cascade – brewed at a point in time when the subject of craft beer and especially aromatic hops was still widely unfamiliar in Germany. The beer is still on the market today – now certified organic and sold under the name Tap 4: Mein Grünes.

A further important milestone that has had a lasting effect on the product portfolio followed in 2007: the first collaboration brew with an American craft-beer brewer on German soil. Garrett Oliver, the master brewer of New York's Brooklyn Brewery, was a long-time friend of owner Schneider and brewer Drexler. After already thinking often about the possibility of a collaboration brew, in 2007 it was finally put into practice. 'At the time it was an experiment with a dearly loved bloke,' Georg Schneider reports. The plan in Kelheim as well as New York would be to brew a hopped wheat beer using the same recipe but with raw materials from their respective continents. 'We had a bet,' Schneider says. 'I was convinced that the results would come out very similar, Garrett the opposite.' It was the American who would be proved right. The two brews were distinctly different in character. Besides the terroir considerations for the hops and malt, this is certainly an indication of the important effect on the aromatics of a weissbier of using local yeasts. The result with the Kelheim brew was so convincing that it became part of the product portfolio, under the name Tap 5: Meine Hopfenweisse. The product that drew shakes of the head from traditionalists when it was introduced has since become established. What's more, the strongly hopped wheat beer has become the standard for a new style of cold-hopped weissbier.

The constant innovation and willingness to experiment of the Schneider and Drexler team manifests itself in many areas. During fermentation, Belgian seasonal yeasts are sometimes added (resulting in an especially dry, completely fermented weissbier), or they experiment with the annual limited-edition Tap X range with storage and maturation in casks. They are proud of their labels. After futile attempts with various design agencies, Georg Schneider, the creative one in the business, finally designed them himself. 'Taste also has an objective component,' he says, 'and the colour choices provide a clue to consumers as to what to expect in the beer.'

It's certainly never easy, but the men from Kelheim succeed well with the balancing act between guarding tradition – Schneiders' original white beer is retained as always, now sold under the name Tap 7: Unser Original – and future-proofing innovations. No wonder – they've had a lot of practice over the years. The first great innovation after all dates back to 1907 and was thanks to Schneider's great grandmother Mathilde: the oldest wheat doppelbock in Bavaria, on the product list today as Tap 6: Unser Aventinus. When we visited, the tasting circle had just sat. At Kelheim beers from all over the world are tasted regularly, to keep their eyes and mind open to new currents and developments in the beer world. Georg Schneider VI promises: 'We're taking even more new paths!'.

THE DNA OF THE BUSINESS WAS ALREADY SO WELL ESTABLISHED THAT WE'RE TAKING NEW RISKS!

S. Ostermeier
WEISSE

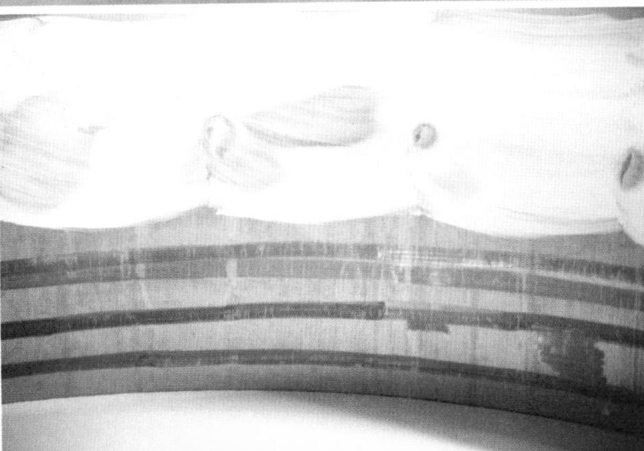

Brick Lane salted meat bagel

BRICK LANE SALTED MEAT BAGEL

Years ago in a Jewish bakery in Brick Lane in London I ate a salted meat 'beigel'. *This specialty of the house is served 24 hours a day there: hot corned beef, in thick slices on a fresh, rather soft bagel, spread thickly with fiercely hot mustard.*

PREPARATION
20 minutes

METHOD

Preheat the oven to 200°C (400°F).

Slice the cabbage as thinly as possible. Marinate the cabbage in the vinegar, olive oil, nut oil, salt and sugar, and knead until soft.

Spray the bagels with water and reheat in the oven for 5 minutes on either side, turning once.

Warm the stock, remove from the heat, add the pastrami slices and set aside to infuse. Halve the bagels crossways, pile high with salad and the drained meat, spread on some mustard and serve immediately.

BEER STYLES: Pale ale, ale, lager, porter . . . many beer styles suit this filled bagel.

SPECIAL RECOMMENDATION: Matching the inspiration for this recipe, a beer from London – the strong, dark IPA Black by Kernel (see p. 65) – a highly successful fusion of typical IPA fruity bitterness with rather atypical toasty malt flavours.

INGREDIENTS
Serves 4

- 350 g (12½ oz) pointed white, savoy, or white cabbage
- 1–2 tablespoons white wine vinegar
- 3 tablespoons olive oil
- 1 tablespoon nut oil
- salt
- pinch of sugar
- 4 sesame seed bagels
- 500 ml (17 fl oz/2 cups) beef stock
- 4 × 8 mm (½ in) slices pastrami* (about 400 g/14 oz)
- dijon mustard

*

Pastrami
(from the Romanian pastrama, *from* pastra = *press, bottle, preserve) is the name of the spiced, salted, smoked and steamed beef from Jewish American cuisine. Romanian migrants brought their traditional recipe to New York, where people loved the juicy, smoky meat, especially in thick open sandwiches, which are becoming ever more popular worldwide.*

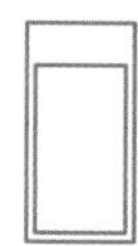

FRIED BLACK SAUSAGE OPEN SANDWICH WITH FRIED EGG AND PARSLEY

Fried black sausage straight from the pan, topped with a fried egg and served on buttered rye bread with hot mustard, accompanied by parsley salad and a strong beer. Our new favourite supper!

INGREDIENTS
makes 4

Dressed parsley
- ½ bunch flat-leaf (Italian) parsley
- a few splashes of aromatic vinegar or white wine vinegar
- 2 tablespoons olive oil
- salt
- freshly ground black pepper

Black sausage open sandwich
- 4 slices gersterbrot* or your favourite bread
- softened butter, for spreading
- hot mustard, for spreading
- 3 tablespoons oil
- 4 × 60–80 g (2–2¾ oz) slices black (blood) sausage suitable for frying (ask your butcher)
- 4 eggs
- salt
- freshly ground black pepper

*

Gersterbrot
is an especially tasty twice-baked sourdough bread made with mixed rye and wheat, particularly beloved in Lower Saxony, Bremen and Hesse.

PREPARATION
20 minutes

METHOD

For the dressed parsley: Wash the parsley in lukewarm water and spin dry. Tear the leaves from the stems into bite-sized pieces. Toss in the vinegar and oil, and season with salt and pepper. Set aside.

Preheat the oven to 80°C (180°F).

For the black sausage open sandwich: Spread the bread slices with butter and mustard. Heat 2 tablespoons of the oil in a non-stick frying pan and fry the black sausage slices quickly for 1–2 minutes on each side.

Keep them warm on a plate in the oven. Heat the remaining oil in the frying pan and break in the eggs. Fry for 4–6 minutes. Season with salt and pepper.

On each plate, top a bread slice with a slice of black sausage and a fried egg, and serve with the parsley salad.

BEER STYLES: Strongly aromatic beers (flavoured with hops, malt or yeast) such as altbier, märzen or a Belgian special.

SPECIAL RECOMMENDATION: Sticke by Uerige, Düsseldorf, Germany (see p. 191). A more strongly brewed variant of the legendary Dusseldorf altbier, with 6 per cent alcohol.

Fried black sausage open sandwich with fried egg and parsley

CHEESEBURGER WITH BEER ONIONS AND MUSTARD KETCHUP

INGREDIENTS
Serves 4

Beer onions
600 g (1 lb 5 oz) onions
2 tablespoons oil
salt
1 garlic clove
large pinch of smoked paprika*
200 ml (7 fl oz) beer
1 tablespoon golden or maple syrup
freshly ground black pepper

Mustard ketchup
60 ml (2 fl oz/¼ cup) tomato ketchup
3 tablespoons wholegrain mustard
1 tablespoon hot mustard

Cheeseburgers
500 g (1 lb 2 oz) coarsely minced (ground) beef (brisket, short ribs and/or chuck steak)
olive oil, for frying
salt
4 slices cheddar
4 burger buns
sliced Danish gherkins, to serve

*

Smoked paprika
is available as Portuguese piménton de la Vera (with a protected designation of origin), in three heat levels: dulce (mild and sweet), agridulce (sweet and hot) and picante (very hot). The art of seasoning with paprika is not to be underestimated – use it carefully.

The shiny gold cheese melts over the fried burger, while beer-braised onions and sweet hot mustard ketchup provide additional taste and spiciness. Another beer with that, please!

PREPARATION
35 minutes

METHOD

For the beer onions: Peel the onions and cut into strips. Heat the oil in a large frying pan over medium heat, add the onion, season with salt and fry for 8–10 minutes until golden brown. Peel and dice the garlic, and add to the pan. Dust with the paprika. Add the beer and golden syrup. Cook, uncovered, until thick. Season with pepper and a little more salt if needed. Keep warm.

For the mustard ketchup: Mix the tomato ketchup with both the mustards. Set aside.

For the cheeseburger: Preheat the oven to 100 °C (210 °F). Shape the meat into four patties. Heat a little oil in a frying pan with a lid and fry the burgers for 2–3 minutes on each side (medium–rare). Season with salt when you turn them over. Top each patty with a slice of cheese, add the lid, remove from the heat and leave for the cheese to melt.

Meanwhile halve the buns crossways, and lay them cut side up on a baking tray lined with baking paper and warm them in the oven for 3–4 minutes. Spread the mustard ketchup on the bottom half of each bun. Lay the patties on top, and gherkin and onion on top of them. Add the top half of each bun and serve the cheeseburgers immediately.

BEER STYLES: Well-hopped strong beers such as ale, altbier, red ale and IPA.

SPECIAL RECOMMENDATION: A classic IPA like Sierra Nevada's (see p. 221) Torpedo Extra, or a slightly less alcoholic PA like the Pale Ale, Amarillo from The Kernel, England.

Cheeseburger with beer onions and mustard ketchup

I'VE ACTUALLY BEEN CONVERTING PEOPLE SINCE THE END OF THE 1980S.

BONN, GERMANY

ALE-MANIA

THE BEDROCK

When we visited Fritz and Heike Wülfing in Bonn, we met in a brewery in a state of new departures – in the truest sense of the words. But new things are already in sight for Ale-Mania.

As we spend the afternoon with master brewer Fritz Wülfing, reviewing the day and enjoying the hearty cheese pancakes he has lovingly made himself, he and his wife Heike are very happy. For what started as a hobby for Fritz, will in the near future become a 'real' brewery with its own brewing facility. In the morning we met them both in Ale-Mania's old space and then travelled to Siegburger Brauhaus, where until now Wülfing has been a guest as a 'brewing cuckoo'. They had just been with the landlord and the planning office to visit the new premises for their brewery and discuss what still needs to be done before they can install their production equipment.

With that, a long history will reach its logical happy ending. At the end of the 1980s, Wülfing began to try making beers that suited his taste. At some point he'd stumbled upon the strongly hopped beers from the American craft-beer scene, which was already in full swing. The beers he was able to try from there impressed him so much that he began to brew as a hobby. Training as a beer sommelier followed.

Wülfing is a real fan of hops. You notice that with your first sip of his beers. And while he has added other beer styles to his brewing portfolio – such as a remarkably fine and original gose but also diverse stouts – his signature brews are without any doubt still his ale and IPA. It's anything but a coincidence that he became famous for these beer styles strongly dominated by hops. 'I only brew beer that tastes good to me personally,' Wülfing says, and in talking about taste, mentions – not without a little playful modesty – 'a certain overlap with other beer drinkers'. That's naturally one way of putting it. But you could also say that his brews are always among the first named when people talk about the best IPAs in Germany.

One factor in the high quality is certainly the long experience Wülfing has had over the years with this style. He was one of the first in Germany to brew IPAs, originally under the name FritzAle, which he had to give up in favour of a soft drink manufacturer with the same first name. He now operates under the brand name Ale-Mania, (Alamannia was the Roman word for Germany). And as before, his IPA is still developing: 'It's

I ONLY BREW BEERS THAT TASTE GOOD TO ME PERSONALLY.

getting better and better!' agrees Jon Brus, from the larger Netherlands brewer de Molen when during our visit there the conversation turned to Wülfing's beer. Today Ale-Mania's beers are carried by a substantial, deeply integrated and anything but superficial bitterness.

Until his own brewing plant is installed in the new premises – largely constructed by Wülfing himself, who is a qualified mechanical engineer – he will continue to be a guest of other breweries. In Peter Esser's Braustelle in the Cologne suburb Ehrenfeld, for example, or also with Ulrich Karl Tröger in his nearby Siegburger Brauhaus. In his own space he hopes to use his lovingly restored old can-closing machine again. A brand-new one would be much too expensive for the brewery, which although professionally run is still a sideline. But the manufacturer to whom he made the enquiry still had an old, discontinued one standing about. And once Wülfing had explained why and for what purpose he needed it, the manufacturer adapted it on the spot.

On the subject of cans, too, Wülfing is a pioneer and – just as he is about craft beer in general – a persuasive evangelist. In his opinion, on qualitative grounds there's nothing better than this medium for holding beer, despite it often being falsely considered inferior. Above all because cans, in contrast with bottles, offer absolute protection against beer's aroma-killer number one: UV light. And the energy balance of aluminium cans – from a recycling point of view – is not nearly as bad. And so – taking into account the final carbonation through can fermentation – Fritz Wülfing uses aluminium, pragmatically and without prejudice, for his Gose in die Dose (gose in the can).

I REALLY LIKE TO COME INTO THE BREWERY IN THE MORNING AND THINK, 'WHAT KIND OF BEER WILL I BREW TODAY?'.

What's also very important to this craft-beer pioneer from Bonn is the collegial and collaborative spirit of the movement. He has already created collaboration brews with many of his colleagues, with Sebastian Sauer from Freigeist or Johannes Heidenpeter from Berlin, for example, and he has supported many young people who've come to him for his knowledge and experience. Not least for this reason, in 2014 he published his own book with his wife Heike – *Brew Your Own Craft Beer: The Homebrewing Revolution*, published by Lampertz. We warmly recommend it to anyone who wants to explore the subject in greater depth or perhaps even get their own brew under way.

40
60
20
80
0
C
100

Pilsnermalz
Weizenmalz
Karamellmalz
Perle
Koriander
Milchsäure
Meersalz
AM
ALE*MANIA
craftbeer
Die Gose
in der Dose
Zutaten:
Wasser,
Gerstenmalz,
Hopfen,
Koriander,
Meersalz,
Milchsäure, Hefe
Biersmarck GmbH
Gerichtsweg 30
53227 Bonn
Mindestens
haltbar bis:
31 März 2016
Dosengärung
14 IBU
12° Plato
Alk. 5,1 % Vol.
℮ 0,33l
www.ale-mania.de

AM
ALE-MANIA
craftbeer
Session IPA
0,33l

AM
ALE MANIA
craftbeer
Die Gose in der Dose
AM
ALE MANIA
craftbeer
Session IPA
AM
ALE MANIA
craftbeer

THE WHOLE BEAST: RABBIT WITH LEEKS, PEARS AND BEER

INGREDIENTS

Serves 4

1 whole rabbit
about 250 g (9 oz) soup vegetables (such as carrot, celery, parsnip and parsley)
1 bay leaf
salt
2 onions
6 garlic cloves
1 teaspoon sugar
250 ml (8½ fl oz/1 cup) pale beer
1 rosemary sprig
2 thyme sprigs
1 thin leek
1–2 small pears
2 tablespoons olive oil
5 g (¼ oz) butter
freshly ground black pepper

Here the whole rabbit is used: the belly flaps and fillets make roulades, and the legs are braised butter-soft at the same time. The liver and kidneys are fried separately.

PREPARATION

30 minutes (plus about 70 minutes to cook)

METHOD

Separate the legs from the rabbit and free the fillets from the bones. Trim the fat and sinew from the organs and refrigerate them. Cut the belly flaps off and cut away and retain the fat. Chop up the bones.

Wash the soup vegetables and slice finely. Put them in a high-sided saucepan with the bones and bay leaf. Add 1 litre (34 fl oz/4 cups) of cold water and a pinch of salt, and bring to the boil. Simmer gently for 20 minutes, skimming off any foam.

Wrap up the fillets in the belly flaps and tie with kitchen twine. Melt the rabbit fat in a flameproof roasting tin on the stove top. Sear the legs all over until golden brown, then add the belly flap roulades. Peel the onions and garlic. Slice the onions, add to the tin with the whole garlic cloves and fry briefly. Add the sugar, season with salt and pour in the beer. Boil, uncovered, for 2 minutes.

Preheat the oven to 200°C (400°F). Pass the rabbit stock through a sieve and measure out 500 ml (17 fl oz/2 cups). Pour the stock in with the rabbit. Add the rosemary and thyme, and transfer the tin to the oven for 30 minutes. Thinly slice the leek then wash thoroughly and drain. Cut the pears into thin wedges and remove the core. Add the leek and pear to the tin, season with salt, stir, then cook for a further 10 minutes.

Meanwhile, halve the kidneys and cut the liver into quarters. Heat the oil in a small frying pan over medium–high heat and quickly fry the kidney and liver pieces. Reduce the heat to medium, add the butter and cook for a further 3–4 minutes. Season with salt and pepper and serve with the rabbit.

BEER STYLES: Wheat beer, pilsner, kölsch.

SPECIAL RECOMMENDATION: Hefeweizen by Live Oak Brewing Company in Austin, Texas, USA – one of the best brews of its style in the United States. Or, if you happen to stumble upon a bottle, Tap 7: Unser Original by Schneider Weisse in Kelheim (see p. 135) is one of the best and most traditional Hefeweizen Germany has to offer.

The whole beast: rabbit with leeks, pears and beer

Veal rissoles with mushrooms

VEAL RISSOLES WITH MUSHROOMS

Seasonal mushrooms in a delicate cream sauce, flavoured with porcini mushrooms and beer, accompanied by rissoles.

PREPARATION

40 minutes

METHOD

Peel and finely dice the onion and garlic. Heat half the butter with 1 tablespoon of the oil in a frying pan, then sauté the onion and garlic until transparent. Pour in half the beer and boil, uncovered, for 5 minutes. Stir in the breadcrumbs, transfer the mixture to a large bowl and set aside to cool. Boil the porcini mushrooms in a saucepan with 400 ml (13½ fl oz) water for 5 minutes, uncovered, then remove from the heat and set aside.

Preheat the oven to 80 °C (180 °F). Add the veal and the egg to the cooled breadcrumb mixture, season with salt and mix until smooth. With wet hands, shape into eight rissoles. Heat the remaining butter with 3 tablespoons of the oil in a large non-stick frying pan over medium heat, then fry the rissoles for 10 minutes, turning now and then. Keep warm on a plate in the oven. Reserve the frying pan with the fat.

For the sauce, peel and finely dice the shallot. Sauté in the rissole fat until transparent. Pour in the remaining beer and boil, uncovered, for 5 minutes. Meanwhile, clean the fresh mushrooms and cut into bite-sized pieces. Strain the porcini and add the soaking liquid to the shallots. Boil for 6–8 minutes to reduce. Add the cream and boil for a further 6–8 minutes until thick.

Meanwhile, heat the remaining oil in another large frying pan over high heat and fry the fresh mushrooms for 6–8 minutes until golden brown (if they release moisture, simply boil it off then continue frying). Transfer the sauce to a high-sided container and purée with a hand-held blender until foamy. Finely chop the parsley and add to the sauce with the fried mushrooms. Season with salt, sugar, pepper and lemon juice. Serve the mushroom sauce with the warm rissoles from the oven.

BEER STYLES: Kölsch, helles, mild pilsner, rotbier, red ale.

SPECIAL RECOMMENDATION: PseudoSue by Toppling Goliath in Decorah, Iowa, USA. A highly complex American Pale Ale with a basket full of tropical fruits, which almost perfectly accompany the tasty combination of cream, veal and mushroom.

INGREDIENTS

Serves 4

1 onion
1 garlic clove
40 g (1½ oz) butter
90 ml (3 fl oz) oil
300 ml (10 fl oz) pale beer
60 g (2 oz) breadcrumbs
10 g (¼ oz) dried porcini mushrooms or mixed dried mushrooms
500 g (1 lb 2 oz) minced (ground) veal
1 egg
salt
1 French shallot
450 g (1 lb) mixed mushrooms (e.g. button, oyster, shiitake mushrooms)
250 ml (8½ fl oz/1 cup) pouring (single/light) cream
a few parsley sprigs
pinch of sugar
freshly ground white pepper
splash of lemon juice

MALT-FLAVOURED

BOCK

Originally a seasonal strong-beer specialty of spring (pale maibock) or autumn–winter. Especially widespread in Bavaria. Intensely high in alcohol and aromatics, with clearly perceptible residual sweetness. Generous and complex on the palate. The name comes from the Lower Saxon town Einbeck.

ORIGIN	Einbeck, Germany
CHARACTER	Maltily sweet, full-bodied
FERMENTATION	Bottom-fermented
ALCOHOL CONTENT	6.5–7.5% Vol. (doppelbock higher)
DRINKING TEMP	8–10°C (46–50°F)
BEST GLASS	Stout glass (brown); Beer tulip (clear)
EXAMPLES	Weltenburger Kloster Asam Bock, Einbecker Ur-Bock
RECIPES	'Pulled Pork' (p. 173), Beer-braised Ribs (p. 189), Beer Jus (p. 181)
VARIANTS	Maibock (May), weihnachtenbock (Christmas) or doppelbock (double); eisbock (ice) and weizenbock (wheat)

SAUSAGES IN AN ONION BROTH

INGREDIENTS

Serves 4

Sausages

600 g (1 lb 5 oz) onions
1 tablespoon mustard seeds
1 teaspoon white peppercorns
8 juniper berries
100 ml (3½ fl oz) mild beer vinegar or white wine vinegar
100 ml (3½ fl oz) pale full beer
salt
1 tablespoon sugar
1 whole clove
2 bay leaves
8 medium sausages
4 parsley sprigs

Horseradish on buttered bread

softened butter, for spreading
4 slices farm-style rye bread, or caraway bread or another favourite bread
salt
a little fresh horseradish

This dish is inspired by the Franconian Blauen Zipfeln *(blue peaks). In the original, authentic Nuremberg sausages are slowly cooked in a hearty onion broth with white wine, vinegar and herbs; during cooking the sausages, which are added raw, blanch and develop the light-blue colour that gives the dish its name.*

PREPARATION

40 minutes

METHOD

For the sausages: Peel the onions and slice into thin rings or strips. Gently bruise the mustard seeds, peppercorns and juniper berries using a mortar and pestle. Bring 800 ml (27 fl oz) water to the boil with the vinegar and beer, and season with salt and pepper. Add the onion, mustard seeds, pepper, juniper berries, clove and bay leaves. Simmer, covered, for 10 minutes. Add the sausages and cook for 20 minutes over medium heat.

For the horseradish on buttered bread: Butter the bread slices and season lightly with salt. Peel the horseradish with a vegetable peeler. Scrape off thin shavings with the back of a knife, or grate finely, and scatter over the buttered bread.

Arrange the sausages in a deep plate with some of the onion broth. Roughly chop the parsley and scatter over the top. Serve with the horseradish bread.

BEER STYLES: Pale full beer and kellerbier, pale wheat beer, kölsch, witbier or gose.

SPECIAL RECOMMENDATION: A beer in the style of a Belgian witbier, such as Hitachino Nest White Ale from Japan, with notes of coriander and orange peel, typical of the style, which subtly supplement the onion broth. An American alternative is Zwickel by Urban Chestnut Brewery in St. Louis, Missouri. A traditional Bavarian style lager, just by the origin of its style, it's the perfect addition to these Bavarian inspired sausages.

Sausages in an onion broth

Risotto with pears, beer, bacon and radicchio

RISOTTO WITH PEARS, BEER, BACON AND RADICCHIO

This delicious risotto melds the flavours of parmesan and bacon with the sweetness of pears, along with the slightly bitter notes of radicchio and beer: simple, refined and good to share.

INGREDIENTS
Serves 4

80 g (2¾ oz) onions
1 garlic clove
60 ml (2 fl oz/¼ cup) olive oil
250 g (9 oz) risotto rice
100 ml (3½ fl oz) beer
50 ml (1¾ fl oz) pear juice
1 litre (34 fl oz/4 cups) hot poultry stock
150 g (5½ oz) streaky bacon
½ small radicchio
2 spring onions (scallions)
2 small williams pears
40 g (1½ oz) butter
60 g (2 oz) freshly grated parmesan
salt
freshly ground white pepper

PREPARATION
35 minutes

METHOD
Peel and dice the onions and garlic. Heat 3 tablespoons of the olive oil in a large saucepan and sauté the onion and garlic with the rice until transparent. Pour in the beer and pear juice and boil down. Add a little of the hot stock. Cook, stirring, until the liquid has almost disappeared. Add a bit more stock and stir until it cooks away. Keep adding stock in this way until the rice is cooked, about 25–30 minutes.

Meanwhile, slice the bacon into strips. Cut the radicchio into bite-sized pieces. Slice the spring onions thinly on the diagonal. Cut each unpeeled pear into six wedges, removing the core.

Heat the remaining olive oil in a frying pan and fry the bacon until crisp. Add the pear pieces and fry for another 1 minute. Add the radicchio, and again cook for another 1 minute. Stir through the spring onion. Don't add salt – the bacon is salty enough.

Stir the butter and two-thirds of the parmesan into the risotto until smooth, then season with salt and pepper. Top with the bacon and pear, scatter over the remaining parmesan and serve.

BEER STYLES: Paler beers with bitter hop notes. Helles, pilsner, pale ale.

SPECIAL RECOMMENDATION: Dortmunder Gold by Great Lakes Brewing in Ohio, USA. This strikes the perfect balance between the hop bitterness and malty body with enough substance to leave its mark in the risotto without ruining it with too much bitterness.

I LOVE BEER – YOU COULD ALSO SAY I LIVE BEER.

HAMBURG, GERMANY

KEHRWIEDER KREATIVBRAUEREI

THE PROTOTYPE

When we visit Oliver Wesseloh at his new site, we meet – not for the first time on this trip – in a brewery on the starting blocks. The 500 litre (130 gallon) brewhouse, which he developed himself from old milk tanks, stands ready. As soon as the last pipes and cables are laid, production can begin . . .

Many players in the craft-beer scene began as hobby brewers, acquiring lots of small-scale brewing expertise and experience over the course of the years, and then, after their first successes and to meet the requests of friends and acquaintances, took the leap and dared to become professional. With Oliver Wesseloh, the brains behind the Kehrwieder Kreativbrauerei, it was different. Wesseloh has a diploma in engineering for brewing technology, and is therefore a qualified pro. And for the family business Kehrwieder – besides Wesseloh, his wife Julia and his mother are working with him on the project – their own brewery in the Harburg quarter of Hamburg is the last leg in a long but logical journey.

He became interested in craft beer – or, as he puts it, 'saw the light' – during his years of travel through the American continents. He was first in the Caribbean, then in South America and from 2010 finally active in Miami, Florida. The last stop left its mark on him most of all: 'The creativity and variety of tastes from American craft brewers made a lasting impression on me.'

When Wesseloh returned to Germany with his family in 2012, he began building the brewery. In the same year he completed training as a beer sommelier, to add to the rather more technical perspective of the engineer the communicative and, above all, more enjoyable viewpoint of the presenter.

His first beer from his own brewery is already becoming a big hit: his Prototyp, a 'pilsner on steroids', as Wesseloh himself describes it, has been met with enthusiasm. The bottom-fermented lager – in craft-beer and microbrewery circles quite a rare style, because it requires cooling and expensive technology during fermentation – is left for seven weeks with aromatic hops and develops during that time a uniquely fine balance between the cool clarity of a pilsner and the fruity aromatic intensity of an ale. Ideal too as a debut in the world of craft beer – a concept whose uncritical uptake from the Americans, Wesseloh sees as not entirely unproblematic. By the American definition of the term 'craft beer', which is based on brewing volume, it follows that almost every brewery in Germany is producing craft beer.

But back to Wesseloh himself: apart from the success of Prototyp, 2013 was also a successful year in a completely unexpected direction. When Wesseloh took part in September 2013 in the world beer sommelier championships – 'actually only to meet colleagues and to exchange ideas,' he says – he was completely surprised to reach the final and was finally elected as the best representative of his craft.

Apart from Prototyp, the best known of Wesseloh's beers must be the IPAs of the SHIPA series. The acronym stands for 'single hop India pale ale'. An IPA therefore, brewed and cold-hopped with a single aromatic hop – which, however, changes all the time – although the recipe is otherwise completely identical. In total eleven different SHIPAs have appeared so far: respectively hopped with Simcoe, Cascade, Amarillo, Hüll Melon, Polaris, Mandarina Bavaria, Ella, Equinox, Azacca, Vic Secret and Mosaic.

It's a unique experimental design for studying the variety of aromatic hops – you could taste them all one after the other. But even if you did want to keep them all, that makes no sense, because a long storage time doesn't agree with all beers. Styles whose effect is strongly based on the hop aromas – such as IPA – age especially quickly, and from the very moment they leave the brewery. An IPA that has been stored for several years still demonstrates only a fraction of its original aromatic variety. In complete contrast are dark, strong beer styles, such as porter or stout, which over a storage period of several years become better and better and more complex. Kehrwieder also has such a storable beer in his brewing program: Imperial Black Prototyp, a Baltic (i.e. bottom-fermented) porter, first brewed for the one-year aniversary of the usual Prototyp. Thanks to its great success, it will be reproduced as soon as his own brewery is up and running. Then there will also be several SHIPAs at the same time, so that they can all be tasted one after the other.

Apart from the beers that are his own responsibility, there's also a variety of collaboration brews. The annual Feuchter Traum (Wet Dream), for example, brewed during the harvest with fresh hops – from field to brewhouse in less than five hours – and produced in cooperation with the Riedenburger Brauhaus; or Franz Ferdinand, a cooperation with Erzbräu from Austria; or, with four other breweries from Hamburg (Blockbräu, Gröninger, Joh. Albrecht and Ratsherren), the reproduced traditional Hamburger Senatsbock. Or You Can Leave Your Hat On, a collaboration brew in the style of a barley wine with Brauhaus Nittenau.

The latest trick is Moll, a collaboration brew with Alexander Himburg from BrauKunstKeller on the occasion of the Braukunst Live! craft-beer fair in Munich. Its organiser, Frank Böer had, in the face of the huge number of ever newer IPAs, promised the brewer a free stand, where he could present a new interpretation of a traditional style. For Wesseloh and Himburg it was incentive enough to put their heads together and develop a new sour smoked beer using an old Berlin recipe, flavoured with roasted mulberry tree chips.

Given the creativity of this Hamburg man, we should all be curious about which exciting experiments the future might bring in his small Harburg brewery tailor-made for experimentation.

THE CREATIVITY AND VARIETY OF TASTES FROM AMERICAN CRAFT BREWERS MADE A LASTING IMPRESSION ON ME.

YOUR
HAT
ON
BARLEY
WINE
PROTO
TYP
WELTMEISTER WEISSE
FRAMBOISE
2014
SHIPA
SHIPA
SHIPA
Equinox

CALF HEART WITH FRIED POTATO

Heart is the most underestimated of all offal. The tender meat can even be prepared like a steak. Add baked potatoes and hollandaise sauce with beer, and you're ready for a very special steakhouse evening at home.

PREPARATION

40 minutes

METHOD

For the fried potato: Peel the potatoes and slice thinly. Peel the onion and slice into thin rings. Heat the clarified butter in a large frying pan and sauté the onion rings until transparent. Remove from the pan and set aside. Spread the potato slices in the pan and fry for 3–4 minutes, then turn them over. Fry for a further 8–12 minutes, turning occasionally, until the potato slices are golden brown. Stir the marjoram leaves and onion into the potatoes. Season with salt. Keep warm.

For the hollandaise sauce: Peel and finely dice the shallot. Bring the beer, beer vinegar, sugar and shallot to boil in a saucepan. Boil until the liquid has reduced to 2 tablespoons, then pass through a sieve.

Melt the butter in a saucepan, bring to the the boil and pour through a fine-mesh sieve. Mix the egg yolks with the beer reduction in a heatproof bowl, add the paprika and whisk over a hot water bath until thick and creamy. Gradually whisk in the butter, drop by drop at first, then in a thin stream. Season with salt. Whip the cream until thick and fold into the sauce just before serving. Season with salt and the extra beer.

For the calf heart: Preheat the oven to 160 °C (320 °F). Cut the heart into three thick pieces, removing the membrane and sinews. Season with salt and pepper. Heat some oil in an ovenproof frying pan and sear the heart pieces all over for 3–4 minutes. Bruise the peeled garlic and add with the thyme. Transfer the pan to the oven and cook the heart for 12 minutes, turning once. Remove from the oven and rest for 3 minutes, then turn and rest for another 3 minutes. Slice and serve.

BEER STYLES: Depending on how you like or tolerate bitterness, a helles, pilsner or even an IPA is recommended. The beer for the sauce shouldn't be too bitter; a Belgian Trappist beer is a good option.

SPECIAL RECOMMENDATION: Two Trappist beers from the seven Trappist breweries worldwide: the rather sweeter Chimay Blue Grande Réserve or the highly complex but unfortunately very rare Orval.

INGREDIENTS

Serves 4

Fried potato

600 g (1 lb 5 oz) boiling potatoes, cooked the day before

1 onion

50 g (1¾ oz) clarified butter (ghee)

½ bunch marjoram, leaves picked

salt

Hollandaise sauce

1 French shallot

100 ml (3½ fl oz) strong beer, plus an extra splash to finish

1–2 tablespoons beer vinegar, or white wine vinegar or tarragon vinegar

pinch sugar

250 g (9 oz) butter

2 medium egg yolks

1 teaspoon sweet paprika

salt

50 ml (1¾ fl oz) thickened (whipping) cream

Calf heart

600 g (1 lb 5 oz) calf heart

salt

freshly ground black pepper

oil, for searing

1 garlic clove

4 thyme sprigs

RIB-EYE STEAK WITH A BALSAMIC BUTTER SAUCE AND BLACKBERRIES

INGREDIENTS
Serves 2

2 × 200 g (7 oz) rib-eye steaks
80 g (2¾ oz) butter
40 g (1½ oz) watercress
100 g (3½ oz) blackberries
2 tablespoons oil
salt
freshly ground black pepper
100 ml (3½ fl oz) strong beer
2 teaspoons mild balsamic vinegar
1 tablespoon sugar

Sweet blackberries lie in a subtly sour balsamic vinegar and butter sauce, seasoned with a suggestion of strong beer, gently caressing the medium-cooked steak. Fresh watercress provides a slight bitterness and pleasant sharpness to this delicious offering.

PREPARATION
25 minutes

METHOD

Take the meat out of the refrigerator a good 2 hours before beginning. It should be at room temperature when you work with it. Preheat the oven to 80°C (180°F) and place a heatproof serving platter in it. Dice the butter finely and freeze on a small plate lined with baking paper. Wash and spin dry the watercress, and tear into rough bite-sized pieces. Rinse the blackberries under hot water.

Heat the oil in a large non-stick frying pan over high heat. Season the steaks with salt and pepper Quickly sear on one side for 2–3 minutes, then turn and fry on the other side for another 2–3 minutes. Transfer to the platter in the oven.

Deglaze the pan with the beer and bring to the boil. Add the balsamic vinegar and sugar, and boil, uncovered, for another 2 minutes. Gradually whisk in the frozen butter cubes. Add the blackberries and toss through. Season with salt and pepper.

Remove the steaks from the oven and stir the juice from the platter into the sauce. Arrange the steaks on serving plates with the sauce and the watercress, and serve immediately.

BEER STYLES: Strong beers high in alcohol, such as doppelbock, dark ales, strong and imperial ales or stouts, particularly barrel-aged beers.

SPECIAL RECOMMENDATION: Velvet Merkin by Firestone Walker Brewing, California, USA. A mighty oatmeal stout, which is aged in bourbon barrels and adds a lot of complexity on the plate.

Rib-eye steak with a balsamic butter sauce and blackberries

Beer-roasted 'pulled pork' with mashed potato and corn

BEER-ROASTED 'PULLED PORK'* WITH MASHED POTATO AND CORN

Sweet corn and mash is a classic of southern American cuisine, available in every diner, usually accompanied by smoked meat. In this version a joint is cooked for hours in beer, until the meat almost falls off the bone as you carve it. With it there's sweet buttered corn and roughly mashed potato with horseradish.

INGREDIENTS

Serves 6

Roast pork

1 garlic clove
2 tablespoons sweet paprika
1 teaspoon smoked salt
1 tablespoon soft brown sugar
1 teaspoon freshly ground black pepper
100 ml (3½ fl oz) beer, plus 2 tablespoons extra for marinating
2 tablespoons olive oil
1 pork neck fillet (about 1.5 kg/3 lb 5 oz)

Mashed potato and corn

1 kg (2 lb 3 oz) roasting potatoes
salt
100 g (3½ oz) butter
100 ml (3½ fl oz) chicken stock
425 g (15 oz) tinned corn, drained
fresh (or bottled) horseradish, to taste

PREPARATION

45 minutes (plus 12 hours to marinate and 6 hours to cook)

METHOD

For the roast pork: Peel and finely dice the garlic and mix with the paprika, smoked salt, sugar and pepper. Rub the extra beer and the olive oil into the pork. Wrap in plastic wrap, sit on a tray and marinate in the refrigerator for 12 hours.

Preheat the oven to 200 °C (400 °F). Drain the meat, sit it on a wire rack in a roasting tin lined with baking paper and cook in the oven for 20 minutes. Reduce the heat to 120 °C (250 °F). Lay the meat on a wire rack or steamer sitting inside a roasting tin with a lid and pour in the beer. Put the lid on and sit the tin in the oven on the lowest shelf. Cook for 6 hours.

For the mashed potato and corn: Peel and boil potatoes and boil in salted water until soft. Drain the potaotes and return to the saucepan. Add 80 g (2¾ oz) of the butter, season with salt and mash using a potato masher or strong whisk.

Melt the remaining butter in a small saucepan and add the chicken stock. Heat the corn up in the chicken stock. Season with salt. Peel the horseradish and shave with the back of a knife. Carve the meat, arrange it on plates with the corn and mashed potato, add a little of the roasting liquid and scatter over the horseradish shavings. Serve immediately.

BEER STYLES: Malt-flavoured beers strong in alcohol, such as bock, doppelbock or weizenbock.

SPECIAL RECOMMENDATION: Uff-da by New Glarus Brewing Company, Wisconsin, USA. A smooth German-style bock, therefore the perfect choice for a mash-up of German-style beer-braised pork and US-sides like corn and mashed potatoes.

*

Pulled-pork sandwiches *are outstandingly good with the meat from this dish. Lightly toast warm burger buns, spread with a little mustard and top with lettuce to your liking. On top of that comes the hot, roughly torn roast meat, sprinkled with tomato ketchup. Add a few fresh apple slices on top and serve immediately.*

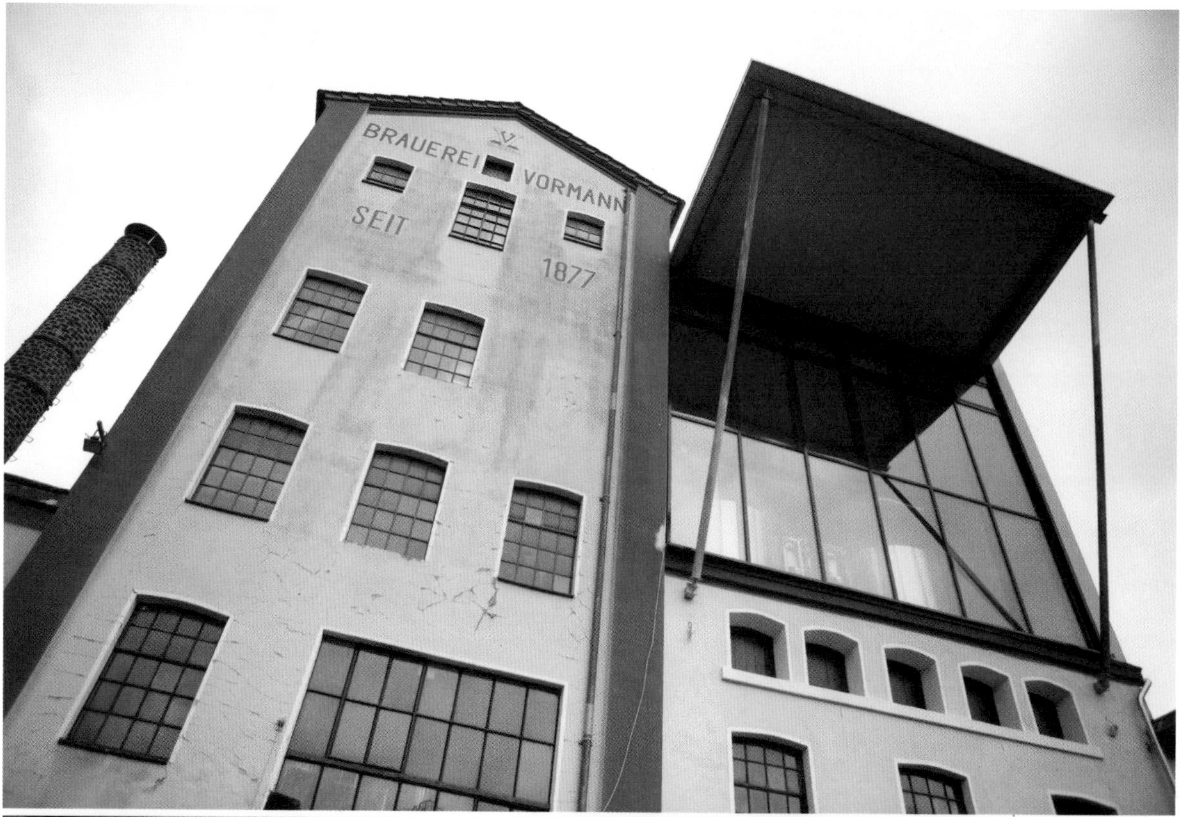
BRAUEREI VORMANN
SEIT 1877

Kühlschiff
8853 L.

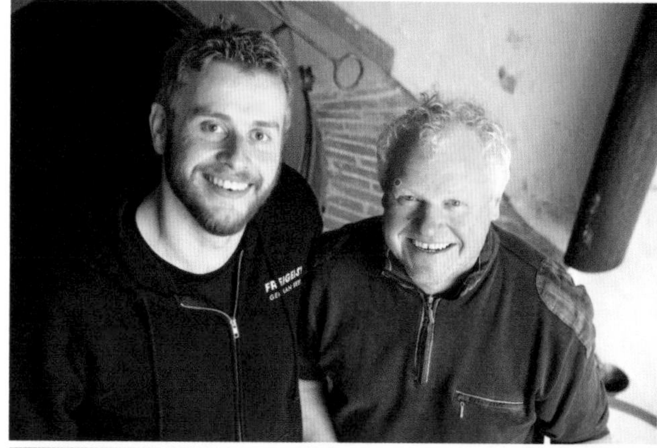

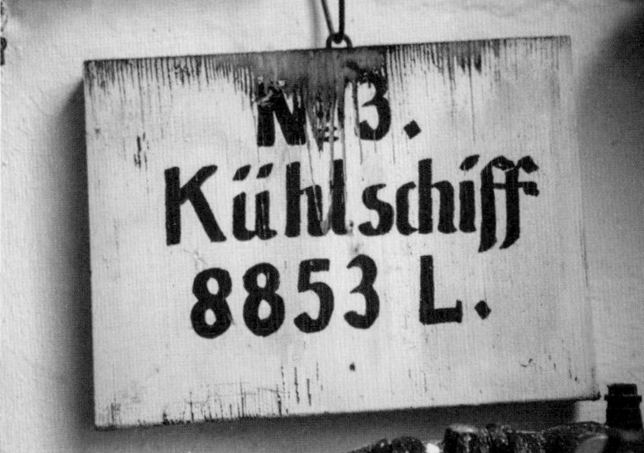

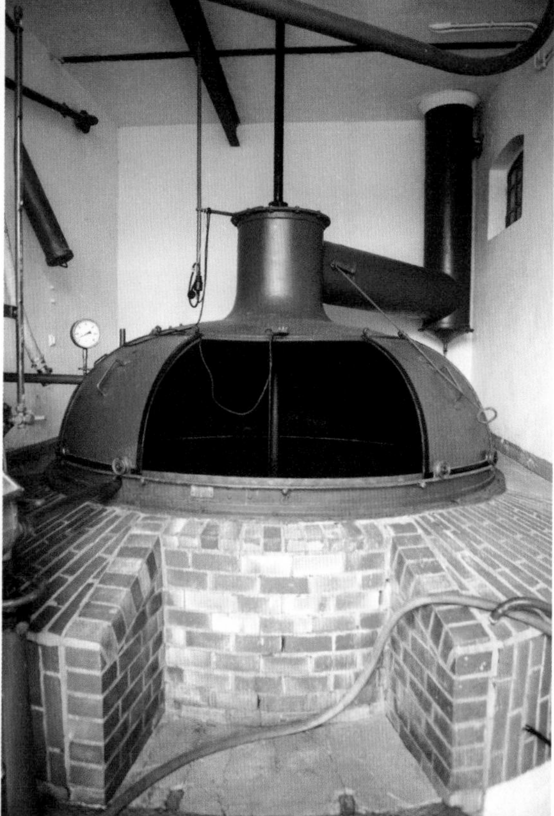

HAGEN, GERMANY

VORMANN

THE HOSTEL WARDEN

Since 1882 the Vormann brewery has found its home on its current site in the Volme valley in Hagen-Dahl. At first glance it's a traditional brewery like many others. And yet in the last few years it has become the place of origin for several extremely interesting craft beers.

As we enter the courtyard of the brewery, a huge pot of potato soup is cooking, lonely and abandoned, on a gas burner. In front of it are benches and two folding trestle tables. There's no sign of the head of the house, nor of his guests. Because today Christian Vormann, master brewer and owner of the brewery, has visitors – as he has had so often in the last few years. Some of the most prominent names in the German craft-beer scene have brewed their beers here in Hagen-Dahl in recent years. The dyed-in-the-wool craft brewer Fritz Wülfing, for example; Philip Overberg from Gruthaus-Brauerei in Münster; or the former world champion sommelier Oliver Wesseloh from Kehrwieder Kreativbrauerei.

This phenomenon is called gypsy brewe-ing. The history behind it is always the same: after the first success as a hobby and small brewer, many craft-beer brewers find that requests from family and friends quickly exceed their homebrewing capacity. Those who don't want to turn their passion straight away into their main source of income, with its associated investments, seek out a brewery with spare capacity the same size as a brewhouse, to reproduce the home-tested recipes in a larger style. Naturally the respective hosts also provide, with their usually long-standing brewing experience, a worthwhile contribution. 'It's always a mutual cross-fertilisation,' says Christian Vormann. Gypsy brewing is one method by which knowhow is exchanged and ideas promoted. Even giants of the international craft-beer scene, such as the Dane Mikkel Borg Bjergsø from the craft-beer legend Mikkeler, brew their beers as nomadic brewers.

Knowledge transfer is also one of the side effects of another very widespread practice in the craft-beer scene: collaboration brews – that is, temporary cooperation between two or more friendly craft-beer brewers. Such joint special brews have a long tradition in the scene. Today Sebastian Sauer from Freigeist Bierkultur is a guest in Hagen, and with him brewers from 2Cabecas in Rio de Janeiro, Brazil, as well as from beer café Teresa's Cafe in Philadelphia. 'Collaboration brews are an excellent opportunity to develop common ideas and concepts and realise them together,' says

Sebastian. Other well-known craft-beer names, for example the Franconian Andreas Gänstaller or Menno Olivier and Jon Brus from de Molen, are also constantly searching for exchanges with friendly colleagues in the form of collaborations.

For Sebastian and his guests from Brazil and the United States, a gose is on the program today, a traditional German sour beer. It's a style that has enjoyed great worldwide popularity among craft-beer aficionados for some time. Here, in its homeland, it still leads a sad existence as a niche product – which by the way also says a lot about the long way the craft-beer movement still has to go here in Germany. Gose is the style in which Sebastian's brewing project Freigeist Bierkultur has busied itself with many variations in the last few years. Sour and salty are the two main aromatic features that mark this beer style, which until the beginning of the twentieth century was widespread, especially in northern and eastern Germany. The Viking Gose from Freigeist, brewed with smoked malt, is very aromatic, as is the Atlantis Gose, which is fermented with oyster shells and seaweed. Sebastian has already brewed with his Brazilian guests a collaborative stout called Rio de Colônia – salted like a gose and fermented with Brazilian Surinam cherries. Today's brew will directly become a gose. More precisely a mango gose fermented with weissbier yeasts – reminiscent of the homeland of the overseas guests.

Christian Vormann, host and fourth-generation brewer in the old family business, is used to this sort of extravaganza. At the moment Peppercorn Weiss is maturing in his tanks, a wheat beer spiced with pepper; or Methusalem, a 10 per cent alcohol, slightly sour and strongly hopped altbier, of the sort that was popular in Dortmund in the mid-nineteenth century. But Vormann also has a few remarkable beers in his own program. His Vormann Vorder is, as he says himself, 'The dream of every modern head brewer'. It's brewed exclusively with the especially aromatic first wort, without being stretched, as is otherwise usual for the improvement of the mash yield, by various second washes with hot water. The result is an intensely aromatic, extract-rich lager in the style of an export. It arose from the wish to brew an especially unusual beer for the turn of the millennium. The recipe was developed, without compromise, only with respect for the taste – 'exactly the way the craft-beer people make it'. For that reason it was originally planned as a once-only brew. The overwhelming success of the deeply malt-flavoured specialty has since ensured that it's still found in the brewery today – despite its above-average price.

Likewise, a remarkable rarity is the malt beer. In contrast to normally available malt *drinks* with less than 0.5 per cent alcohol by volume, the few remaining true malt *beers* are 1.5 per cent alcohol. This one is fermented with yeast and has a much fuller, rounder taste profile. And Vormann's 8 per cent alcohol doppelbock is also a top-flight beer. It was all brewed in a 3,000 litre (790 gallon) unit from 2011. The old brewhouse dating from 1938 is at the moment standing unused in the next building. Just like the copper coolship oustide the door. For Christian Vormann there's no question of giving it up for scrap. That the two will both be reactivated appears not to be precluded, given the way of life that reigns at the moment in Hagen-Dahl.

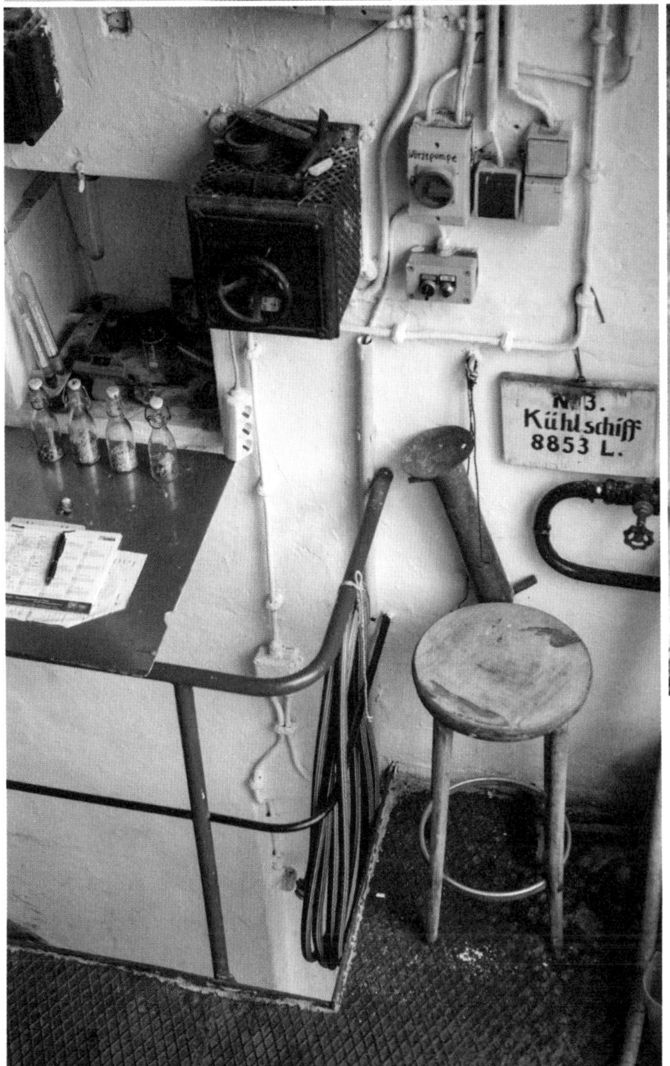

THE FIRST ONE WHO BREWED HIS OWN BEER HERE, IN 1995, WAS FROM A BIKE SHOP IN KIERSPE!

2CABECAS
MUNCHHAUSEN

Vormann
Privat-Brauerei
Vormann
Hagen-Dahl
Sauerländer Weizenbier
Gebraut nach dem Reinheitsgebot
FREIGEIST BIERKULTUR

BEER JUS

This sauce is the diamond of cooking, my grandfather used to say, and this strongly aromatic jus of beef bones, roast vegetables, herbs, spices and beer should confirm his statement.

PREPARATION

About 3 hours (plus time to cool and infuse)

METHOD

Preheat the oven to 225°C (440°F). Wash the soup vegetables and chop roughly. Cut the unpeeled onions into rough pieces. Mix the bones with the vegetables and the oil in a flameproof roasting tin and put in the oven. Roast for 1 hour.

Remove the tin from the oven and place on the stove top. Add the caraway, coriander and mustard seeds, brown sugar, bay leaves, mushrooms (if using) and garlic cloves to the roasted vegetables and deglaze with the beer. Cook, uncovered, for 10 minutes. Pour in the stock and bring to the boil. Skim off any foam with a skimmer.

Return the tin to the oven, reduce the heat to 200°C (400°C) and cook for 2 hours. Remove from the oven and allow to cool completely in the tin on a wire rack (preferably overnight).

Gently remove the congealed fat from the top – under it twinkles the slightly gelled jus. Strain this rich stock and season to taste with salt and pepper.

TIP: The rich stock can be frozen in portions. It makes a great base for cream sauces and goes well with roasts, sausages and steaks. It's also particularly good for a classic of northern German leftover cooking: Hamburger rundstück warm*.

BEER STYLES: Mildly hopped Bavarian or Franconian dark beer, bock, black beer.

SPECIAL RECOMMENDATION: Black Bavarian by Sprecher Brewing Company in Wisconsin, USA. A dark German-style lager which gives the jus a nice, dark colour and some sweetness without leaving too much bitterness.

INGREDIENTS

Makes about 800 ml (27 fl oz)

about 500 g (1 lb 2 oz) soup vegetables (such as carrot, leek, celery, parsnip and parsley)
4 onions
1 kg (2 lb 3 oz) meaty beef bones
60 ml (2 fl oz/¼ cup) vegetable oil
1 teaspoon caraway seeds
1 teaspoon coriander seeds
1 teaspoon mustard seeds
2 tablespoons soft brown sugar
2 bay leaves
5–10 g (¼ oz) dried porcini mushrooms (optional)
2 garlic cloves
500 ml (17 fl oz/2 cups) dark beer
1.5 litres (51 fl oz/6 cups) beef stock
salt
pepper

*

Hamburger rundstück warm *is a northern German Monday meal, in which the remains of the Sunday roast are warmed in gravy (never boiled!). The meat is served with gherkins in bread rolls (the 'round piece'). The bread can also be spread with mustard and/or butter. It tastes best when the gravy has already soaked into the bread slightly.*

RILLETTES

INGREDIENTS
Serves 4–6

800 g (1 lb 12 oz) pork belly
about 1.5 litres (51 fl oz/ 6 cups) beef stock
2 bay leaves
2 French shallots
1 garlic clove
500 g (1 lb 2 oz) butter
1 teaspoon fennel seeds
4 summer savoury sprigs
salt
freshly ground black pepper

For French rillettes, meat is cooked in its own spiced fat and then, when butter-soft, pressed into it. I cook the meat in stock and then preserve it in herb butter – the elegant spread is then ready for supper or a buffet.

PREPARATION
20 minutes (plus 2 hours to cook and 2 hours to cool)

METHOD
Remove the fat from the pork belly and set aside. Cover the belly with the stock in a stockpot, cover and bring to the boil. Remove the white foam with a skimmer. Add the bay leaves and fat, then cover and simmer gently for 2 hours.

Peel and finely dice the shallots and garlic, and put in a saucepan over medium heat with the butter. Add the finely chopped summer savoury. Melt the butter and allow it to bubble up. Season with salt and pepper.

Remove the pork from the cooking juices and tear it into strips of your preferred fineness using two forks. Add to the butter, season again with salt and pepper if necessary, and boil up again. Fill sterilised preserving jars with the pork mixture while still hot, then seal and allow to cool.

TIPS: Tastes very good on rustic bread, served with freshly cut onion rings and cornichons.

Rillettes keep in a sealed jar in the refrigerator for up to 1 month.

BEER STYLES: Dunkel, black beer, pale ale, IPA, stout, but also strongly hopped pilsner.

SPECIAL RECOMMENDATION: Pork fat, butter, onions, garlic – the fatter the dish, the more you need some bitterness for the balance. Choose a top IPA or Imperial IPA like Pliny the Elder from Russian River Brewing Company, California, or Focal Banger from The Alchemist in Vermont, USA.

Rillettes

SOUR BEER

GOSE

The most widespread beer style in northern Germany before pilsner took over. The basis is a white beer fermented by lactic acid bacteria, lightly hopped and spiced with coriander (cilantro) and salt. Subtly refreshing in summer and a great accompaniment to food. The craft-beer movement has rediscovered the old style.

ORIGIN	Goslar, Germany
CHARACTER	Sour and fresh, aromatic with spice, salty
FERMENTATION	Top-fermented, with lactic acid fermentation
ALCOHOL CONTENT	4–7% Vol.
DRINKING TEMP	5–9°C (41–48°F)
BEST GLASS	Beer tulip; American wheat-beer glass
EXAMPLES	Ale-Mania Gose, Original Döllnitzer Ritterguts Gose, Freigeist's Viking Gose
RECIPES	Fried Little Fish (p. 27), Smoked Herring (p. 106), Sprats (p. 42), Mussels in Beer (p. 91), Sausages in an Onion Broth (p. 158), Venison Schnitzel (p. 131)
VARIANTS	Gose with smoked malt, with rhubarb or quince, with spruce needles or even with oysters and seaweed (Freigeist's Atlantis Gose). Closely related to other sour beers, such as gueuze, lichtenhainer, grodziskie or wheat beer.

CAVOLO NERO WITH CARAMELISED POTATOES AND TYROLEAN HAM

INGREDIENTS
Serves 4

Caramelised potatoes
800 g (1 lb 12 oz) small potatoes
salt
60 ml (2 fl oz/¼ cup) oil
1–2 tablespoons sugar
20 g (¾ oz) butter
salt

Cavolo nero
800 g (1 lb 12 oz) cavolo nero*
salt
2 French shallots
1 garlic clove
3 tablespoons olive oil
20 g (¾ oz) butter
freshly ground black pepper
pinch of sugar
200 g (7 oz) thinly sliced Tyrolean ham**

*

Cavolo nero
also known as black kale or Tuscan kale, has long been grown in Italy and Portugal. The leaves are more tender and much less bitter than kale, but still flavoursome and quick to cook. A worthwhile discovery! Try it in pasta with chilli or as a side dish with sausages or cutlets.

**

Tyrolean ham
is a juniper-flavoured ham that originated in Tyrol, Italy. Look out for it in Italian delicatessens.

This dish is inspired by the hearty northern German grünkohlessen, *in which pork belly is boiled with kale and served with sweet baked potatoes. In this elegant version, mild cavolo nero* is only lightly steamed and served with Tyrolean ham**. The caramelised potatoes remain.*

PREPARATION
45 minutes

METHOD
For the caramelised potatoes: Peel the potatoes with a vegetable peeler and boil in salted water for 10–15 minutes, depending on their size, until just cooked. Pour off the water and leave to steam dry. Heat the oil in a frying pan and fry the potatoes until brown all over. Add the sugar and, stirring constantly for 2–3 minutes, allow it to caramelise. Add the butter and let it foam up. Season with salt and keep warm.

For the cavolo nero: Remove the cavolo nero leaves from the thick stalks and wash in warm water. Cook in plenty of boiling salted water for 4 minutes.

Remove from the pan and plunge into cold water to cool. Peel and finely dice the shallots and garlic. Drain the cavolo nero and squeeze to remove as much water as possible.

Heat the oil and butter in a frying pan over medium heat, then sauté the shallots and garlic until transparent. Add the cavolo nero and fry for 5 minutes. Season with salt, pepper and sugar. Serve with the Tyrolean ham and caramelised potatoes.

BEER STYLES: Pilsner, helles, export (strong), lager, amber ale.

SPECIAL RECOMMENDATION: The 5AM Saint by Brewdog, Scotland. A full, malty, caramelish body, but at the same time light enough to leave the cabbage and ham its room.

Cavolo nero with caramelised potatoes and Tyrolean ham

Beer-braised ribs with apple sauerkraut

BEER-BRAISED RIBS WITH APPLE SAUERKRAUT

It's hard to believe that meaty ribs prepared this way aren't an American invention, but rather a traditional dish from Hesse, a state in the centre of Germany. Knowing this, it's not surprising that these butter-soft beer-braised ribs go best of all with a fruity apple and beer sauerkraut.

PREPARATION

80 minutes

METHOD

For the beer-braised ribs: Cut the ribs into pieces between every second rib. Heat the oil in a stockpot on the stove top and sear the ribs until brown all over.

Meanwhile, peel and dice the onions and garlic. Remove the browned ribs from the pot. Brown the onion and garlic in the pork fat left in the pot. Add the spices and fry briefly.

Return the ribs to the pot. Stir in the beer and bring to the boil. Add the stock and golden syrup. Season with salt and pepper. Cover and simmer gently for 60 minutes, moving the ribs around now and then.

For the apple sauerkraut: Peel the onion and slice into strips. Heat the oil in a saucepan and sauté the onion until transparent. Add the sauerkraut and cook for 1 minute. Add the sugar, bay leaves and juniper berries. Pour in the beer and apple juice. Bring to the boil then add the stock. Season with salt and gently simmer, covered, for 20 minutes. Cut the apple into quarters, then in slices and add to the sauerkraut with the butter. Simmer, uncovered, for a further 5 minutes.

BEER STYLES: Brown or Scotish ale, märzen, bock.

SPECIAL RECOMMENDATION: Rogue's Dead Guy Ale from Portland, Oregon, USA, with its nice balance of subtle sweet maltiness and hop-driven bitterness.

INGREDIENTS

Serves 4

Beer-braised ribs

1 kg (2 lb 3 oz) meaty pork ribs
60 ml (2 fl oz/¼ cup) oil
2 onions
1–2 garlic cloves
1 teaspoon caraway seeds
1 teaspoon fennel seeds
1 tablespoon sweet paprika
200 ml (7 fl oz) black beer or dark beer
300 ml (10 fl oz) beef stock
2 tablespoons golden or maple syrup
salt
freshly ground black pepper

Apple sauerkraut

1 large onion
2 tablespoons oil
500 g (1 lb 2 oz) sauerkraut*
2 tablespoons soft brown sugar
2 bay leaves
3 juniper berries
100 ml (3½ fl oz) pale beer
100 ml (3½ fl oz) apple juice
400 ml (13½ fl oz) beef stock
salt
1 apple
40 g (1½ oz) butter

*

Sauerkraut

comes in tins or glass jars at the supermarket, green grocer or delicatessen. But try finding artisan versions at organic stores or farmer's markets. They often taste much milder, and are generally more roughly cut and have more bite – so it's worth it!

DÜSSELDORF, GERMANY

UERIGE

THE COMPLETE WORK OF ART

'Craft Beer since 1862', shines the sign from one of the windows. You can argue about whether it's appropriate to describe Uerige Alt with the attribute 'craft'. What's certain is that here in the historic centre of Düsseldorf the same committed striving for uncompromising quality prevails as among its craft-beer colleagues.

'Watch out that you make it under that staircase in one piece, dear!' – the legendary rustic charm of the Köbesse (traditional beer waiters) doesn't stop even for the elegantly dressed older ladies of the Düsseldorf historical society. Two of them have just made their way under the stairs towards the toilets – accompanied by the good wishes of the waiter dressed in traditional blue.

We're sitting with Mr and Mrs Doosch (pronounced 'Doorsht', like 'thirst' in German), two life-sized concrete sculptures in the brewery courtyard, one of the nine new spaces in total where the top-fermented altbier is served. Uerige is always one of the first names dropped when those in the know are asked where the best altbier in Düsseldorf is sold. Beer has been brewed here since 1862, and the building functioned as a guesthouse for a good 100 years before that. But we can't actually admit that with this Düsseldorf institution we're dealing with craft beer in the modern sense, even if the neon sign in the window claims the opposite.

In view of the outstanding quality of the beers in front of us, however, it's an extremely idle observation. It's said that with Uerige altbier it always takes one or two glasses to get used to its strongly hopped style – they use the classic hop cultivars Hallertauer, Spalter and Perle. 'With our bitterness it's a bit like the heat of horseradish,' says the brewery's technical manager, Christoph Tenge. 'It's also only on the palate a short time and then quickly vanishes – in contrast to the heat of chilli, which lasts for ages.' A useful comparison. For us – whose palates have been hardened by many IPAs during our research – it tastes great from the first glass onwards.

'We're still a true house brewery,' Tenge explains. 'With us the malt comes through the door and leaves as finished beer in bottles or barrels.' All the other steps in between are carried out right here in the headquarters – he emphasises this point. The malt used is up to 90 per cent pilsner malt, supplemented with a little caramel malt and roasted malt for a dark copper-shining colour and aromatic depths. It's fermented here by their own yeasts, which are rejuvenated several times during the year by raising them again from their cultures. Altbier is – just like the beer of their eternal rival a few kilometres further up the Rhine, Cologne – top-fermented, and the name refers to this 'old' brewing style compared with that used for pilsner, which was more widespread at the end of the nineteenth century. After the triumph of pilsner, altbier and kölsch are the only two remaining traditional beer styles based purely on barley malt that are still brewed top-fermented in Germany. The two are therefore closely related to each other, which in turn is now not without a certain irony, given the constant fierce trench warfare once waged over which beer was superior.

We don't want to allow ourselves any prejudice on this subject. You could say for certain, however, that the altbier, with its hop flavours and share of roasted malt, is as a rule a more complex, multilayered beer. Kölsch, by contrast, is – just because of its more restrained hopping – in the first moment usually more approachable.

But back to Uerige's 'leckere Dröppke' (tasty little drop), in the words of its own advertising. The 'bitterest beer in Germany' is, the brewery says, brewed in the traditional manner, right up to the imposing copper coolship in the attic. After cooling in this large flat bath, a further cooling process follows in the open vertical cooler, during which the oxygen necessary for the next fermentation process enters the cooling wort. It's also made of copper, and is as beautiful as a sculpture, especially when the wort sparkles as it runs over the cooling fins. At many points during the brewery tour you notice the special dedication and passion the people at Uerige devote to their creations. And the two brew kettles, naturally also of copper (although the insides have long been high-grade steel), and the air-conditioned hop store with its small coloured lighting installation, also bear witness to that.

Essentially, what's served in Uerige is its own altbier. Certainly the wheat beer and draught beer also brewed here are served by the Köbesse with the gesture of a blessing. The bar is also very conscious of tradition – the beer comes not from modern beer taps but is instead tapped from heavy old wooden kegs. Twice a year no altbier flows from the brass beer taps. On the third Thursday every January and October, the so-called sticke alt days, sticke – a somewhat more strongly brewed and hopped variant of altbier with at least 6 per cent alcohol – is served. According to legend it came into being when the master brewer was once too generous with his measurements of malt and hops. What was christened 'stickum' (more or less 'calm and quiet') was explained with hand over mouth and so the special brew got its name. Since then it has become a legend. So much so that on the days it's served, people from all over the world travel there – the 'sticke warriors'.

Thanks to the interest that altbier and sticke alt have also encountered in the United States, in 2005 another beer joined the master brewer's list, which has since become legendary: the even stronger doppelsticke alt (double sticke alt), with 8.5 per cent alcohol. Originally brewed exclusively for export at the request and prompting of the United States importers, the few bottles that have been tried here in Germany have likewise been met with bright enthusiasm. No wonder: the doppelsticke alt is Uerige altbier squared, an aromatic, highly complex, intensely aromatic masterpiece. Which even now that, fortunately, it's sold here in the German market, still remains very rare. The few batches of it that are produced are sold out within the shortest possible time.

HERE THE OWNER IS ALSO A KNOWLEDGEABLE BREWER.

UERIGE
3177

Craft Beer
Seit 1862

Uerige

dat leckere Dröppke
Uerige
Düsseldorf-Altstadt

Schnapsgenuß
während des Bierkonsums
ist hier untersagt
(es stört Jhre Gesundheit
und mein Geschäft.)
DER WIRT

Beer onions

BEER ONIONS

For this classic of Franconian beer cuisine, large onions are filled with thick tasty sausages and braised in the oven in an onion and beer sauce. Bam!

INGREDIENTS
Serves 4

4 very large onions
400 g (14 oz) thick sausages
2 tablespoons oil
1 teaspoon caraway seeds
1–2 teaspoons sweet paprika
1 teaspoon sugar
150 g (5½ oz) dark beer
350 ml (12 fl oz) beef stock
salt
4 marjoram sprigs, or large pinch of dried marjoram
20 g (¾ oz) cold butter
freshly ground black pepper

PREPARATION
30 minutes (plus 60 minutes to roast)

METHOD
Peel the onions and trim the bottoms so they can stand. Cut a little lid off each onion and, using a knife, carefully hollow out the middle until three layers remain. Finely dice the lids, and separately slice the onion removed from the insides into strips. Push the sausage meat out of the skins and mix with the finely diced onion. Fill the onion shells with this mixture.

Preheat the oven to 180°C (350°F). Heat the oil in a flameproof roasting tin on the stove top and fry the onion strips until brown. Stir in the caraway seeds, paprika and sugar. Pour in the beer. Bring to the boil then add the stock.Season with salt. Stand the onions next to each other in this braising liquid (you may need to use the onions to support each other so they hold their shape). Transfer to the oven and bake for 60 minutes, basting the onions now and then with the liquid.

Before serving, roughly chop the marjoram and cut the butter into cubes. Sit the onions on warmed plates. Bring the cooking juices to the boil on the stove top and add the marjoram and cold butter, stirring until the butter is melted. Season to taste if necessary with more salt, sugar and pepper, then pour over the stuffed onions.

BEER STYLES: Dark, malt-flavoured beers such as dark beer, bock, dark wheat beer, red ale.

SPECIAL RECOMMENDATION: The Belgian Abbey Dubbel Chimay Rouge or even the slightly stronger Bleue – both perfect to cook with and accompany the dish as well.

CHEESE STICKS TWO WAYS

INGREDIENTS
Serves 4

400 g (14 oz) frozen puff pastry in sheets
1 egg, lightly beaten
50 g (1¾ oz) grated cheddar
caraway seeds, to taste
50 g (1¾ oz) blue cheese

The quick snack for your favourite beer: crisp, warm puff pastry sticks with cheddar and blue cheese.

PREPARATION
30 minutes

METHOD

Preheat the oven to 220 °C (430 °F). Lay the frozen pastry sheets beside each other on a clean work surface and allow to thaw.

Brush with the beaten egg. Scatter the grated cheese and caraway seeds over half the pastry sheets. Scatter the finely crumbled blue cheese over the remaining sheets. Press on the cheeses lightly.

<u>For cheese sticks:</u> Slice the sheets into strips 1–2 cm (½–¾ in) wide. Hold both ends and twist in opposite directions. Lay the sticks on a baking tray lined with baking paper.

<u>For cheese rounds:</u> Starting at a long side, roll up the sheets and cut into 5 mm–1 cm (¼–1 inch)wide slices. Lay the rounds on a baking tray lined with baking paper.

Bake the sticks and rounds for 12–15 minutes until golden brown.

AN EXTRA SPECIAL RECOMMENDATION: Very different beers go with this snack. We therefore recommend that you simply grab your current favourite beer.

For our photographer, Daniela Haug, this would be, for example, a Westvleteren 12. Not because the really rare Trappist beer enjoys a reputation as the 'world's best beer', but because with its harmonious play of sweet and sour it's one of the most balanced and elegant beers she has ever drunk.

The recipe author, Stevan Paul, would reach for Buddelship's Mitschnagger Pilsener from his hometown Hamburg – because with its flavour and character it's enjoyable all evening, never becoming too much. It's also ideal for craft-beer newcomers.

Finally, Torsten Goffin would open a Triple Seven IPA from the Lower Rhine's Brauprojekt 777, because it delights again and again with its aromatic depths and perfect balance between hop bitterness and dry floral aromatics.

Cheese sticks two ways

Beer bread

BEER BREAD

Good bread takes time. The dough must mature, the bread should bake in peace. But beer bread requires very little work; it only takes about 5 minutes to prepare the dough. The rest is patience – which will be rewarded with a hearty, tasty beer loaf.

INGREDIENTS

Makes about 1 kg (2 lb 3 oz)

150 ml (5 fl oz) malt beer
1 teaspoon sugar
10 g (1/4 oz) fresh yeast
800 g (1 lb 12 oz/5 1/3 cups) plain (all-purpose) flour, plus extra for dusting
1 tablespoon salt

PREPARATION

5 minutes to prepare the dough, 12 hours to rise and about 2 hours 30 minutes to bake

METHOD

Heat 500 ml (17 fl oz/2 cups) of water to lukewarm in a saucepan with the malt beer and sugar. Remove from the heat and mix in the yeast. In a large bowl, loosely knead the flour and salt into the yeast liquid. Don't do this too thoroughly – the yeast will take over in the coming hours and turn it into smooth dough – but there shouldn't be any flour lumps left.

Cover the bowl with plastic wrap and leave the dough at room temperature for 12 hours to mature.

Preheat the oven to 200°C (400°F) and warm a cast-iron casserole pot you, in which you will bake the bread.

Turn the dough out onto a floured work surface. Dust your hands with flour and fold the flattened dough into three like a business letter. Then fold the left and right sides underneath to make an elastic ball.

With flour-dusted hands put the dough in the hot pot. Add the lid and put it in the oven.

Remove the lid after 90 minutes then bake for a further 50–60 minutes until it has a lovely crust. Remove from the oven, allow to cool completely on a wire rack in the pot, and only then remove and slice – preferably using a bread knife – and enjoy.

SOUR BEERS

LAMBIC, GUEUZE

Spontaneously fermented in wooden barrels (i.e. with only wild yeasts from the surrounding air), and thus in the original style beer was made. Gueuze is additionally bottle-fermented. Distinctly sour and with highly complex aromatics from the wild yeasts. Lambic is almost without fizz, while gueuze has Champagne-like bubbles. Whichever way, their low bitterness makes them perfect for cooking.

ORIGIN	Belgium
CHARACTER	Sour, fresh, aromatic
FERMENTATION	Spontaneously fermented (with *Brettanomyces*, etc.)
ALCOHOL CONTENT	4–8% Vol.
DRINKING TEMP	5–9°C (41–48°F)
BEST GLASS	Balloon glass; American wheat-beer glass
EXAMPLES	Cantillon's lambics and Gueuze, Boon's Mariage Parfait, Girardin's 1882 (Black Label)
RECIPES	Smoked Herring (p. 106), Scallops (p. 98), Mussels in Beer (p. 91), Beer-braised Pork Belly (p. 116)
VARIANTS	Fruit lambic, faro. Closely related to gose, lichtenhainer, grodziskie and wheat beer.

STILTON WITH BLOOD ORANGE

INGREDIENTS
Serves 4

2–3 blood oranges
½ pomegranate (see Tips)
200 g (7 oz) stilton
freshly ground black pepper
honey, for drizzling
olive oil, for drizzling

Sometimes great food simply means combining a few perfect products. So, for example, a ripe stilton with blood oranges, olive oil, black pepper, honey and pomegranates yields an unbelievably aromatic, multifaceted taste experience. That was actually just the recipe!

PREPARATION
10 minutes

METHOD

Peel the blood oranges, making sure to also remove the white pith.

Cut the blood oranges into slices. Extract the juicy seeds from the pomegranate; this is best done over the sink, as it will squirt quite a bit.

Roughly break up the stilton, toss with the orange slices and pomegranate seeds, season with pepper and drizzle over honey and olive oil.

TIPS: Rye bread, wholemeal (whole-wheat) bread or pumpernickel bread suit this dish.

In good supermarkets green grocers should have pomegranates during their season (and often beyond), which is during winter.

BEER STYLES: Witbier, honey beer.

SPECIAL RECOMMENDATION: Bloody 'Ell by Beavertown Brewery, London, England. The blood orange juice and zest it was brewed with build up a perfect aromatic bridge to the fruit on the plate, while the IPA aromas are strong enough to counterpart the stilton's intensity.

Stilton with blood orange

Cheese terrine wrapped in leek

CHEESE TERRINE WRAPPED IN LEEK

This elegant dish comes direct from the sophisticated cuisine of the 1980s, a worthwhile little craft project that deserves to be rediscovered. This terrine of two cheeses in a coat of leek is not only a creamy treat – it also looks better now than it did back then!

INGREDIENTS
Makes about 12 slices

1 thick leek
salt
4 leaves gelatine
400 g (14 oz) cream cheese
250 g (9 oz) blue cheese
250 g (9 oz) soft or firm goat's cheese roll
100 ml (3½ fl oz) beer
a few large basil leaves
a few blue or red grapes
20–40 g (¾–1½ oz) frisée

PREPARATION
20 minutes (plus 3 hours to cool)

METHOD
Trim the ends off the leek, separate the leaves and wash them. Boil for 4 minutes in salted water. Remove from the water and plunge into cold water to cool. Drain and dry next to each other between clean tea towels (dish towels). Soak the gelatine in cold water. Separately mix half the cream cheese each into the blue cheese and goat's cheese.

Line a loaf (bar) tin or terrine tin with plastic wrap, then line the tin with the leek leaves so that they are just overlapping and there is enough hanging over the sides to fold over the top later. Warm the beer, squeeze out the gelatine and dissolve it in the beer. Divide this liquid between each of the two cheese mixtures and quickly mix using an electric mixer.

Put the goat's cheese mixture in the tin and smooth the top. Lay the basil leaves on top and press. Add the blue cheese cream and smooth the top. Fold the leek over it and press lightly, cutting off any overhang with scissors. Refrigerate the terrine for at least 3 hours.

Turn the terrine out onto a board, remove the plastic wrap, and slice using a knife dipped in hot water. Garnish with the grapes and frisée.

TIP: Baguettes or a rustic bread go well with this dish, as do hot new potatoes.

BEER STYLES: Witbier or blanche, or alternatively sour beer.

SPECIAL RECOMMENDATION: Damm Inedit, a luxury beer brewed in the style of a Belgian witbier, with wheat, coriander and orange peel, developed by Estrella Damm and top chef Feran Adrià in 2008 for the latter's own high-end kitchen.

BROUWERIJ
DE MOLEN

BROUWERIJ
DE MOLEN

CU Again 4% €2,90
Op & Top
Vuur & Vlam
Dag & Dauw
Amarillo 9,2% €4,75
Heen & Weer 9,2%
Groot & Sterk
Tsarina Esra
Rasputin Bourbon barrel

BROUWERIJ

CAN

BODEGRAVEN, NETHERLANDS

BROUWERIJ DE MOLEN

GUTS AND GLORY

The name-giving windmill stands within sight of the current brewery – although as a site for production it has long been too small. But the men of action John Brus and Menno Olivier would also like to extend the modern spaces once more.

About a 30 minute drive from Amsterdam, in the small Dutch village Bodegraven, lies the home of this European brewing success story. 'Almost every weekend we're on our way to somewhere in Europe for a festival or a beer festival!' explains co-owner John Brus with a sigh, 'And that's each of us at a different one!' 'Us' also means, besides the computer scientist who arrived on the scene in 2009, Menno Olivier, who – exactly like Brus and many others in the craft-beer scene – first began as a hobby brewer. And, once the passion for brewing hit, after years of positions in different breweries, ending with the Stadsbrouwerij de Pelgrim in Rotterdam, he finally brewed himself up as the founder of his own brewery.

A highly successful one, to put it mildly. Because de Molen, the brewery with the conspicuous tendency towards Jane Austen–style double names – translated, the beers are called, for example, Big & Strong, Hammer & Sickel, Hell & Damnation and Bombs & Grenades – enjoys a reputation among craft-beer fans as great as that of Phar Lap, Shergar or Sea Biscuit. In Bodegraven they brew the whole palette of modern craft beer: from Hop & Liefde (Hope & Love), a pale ale with 4.5 per cent alcohol, to a remarkably elegantly hoppped IPA called Vuur & Vlam (Fire & Flame), to sour beer, porter and stout and their strong versions – everything is represented.

But it's with its dark strong beers especially that de Molen has garnered its well-deserved legendary reputation. On the well-known rating platform of the craft-beer scene Ratebeer (www.ratebeeer.com), it was already among the ten best breweries worldwide, but then came numerous other prizes and honours for beers such as the 10 per cent alcohol imperial stout Hel & Verdoemenis (Hell & Damnation) or the 15 per cent alcohol barley wine Bommen & Granaten (Bombs & Grenades; probably few beer names describe so fittingly as this one what awaits the drinker). The variants additionally matured in wooden barrels – for example Bommen & Granaten or the equally legendary Rasputin – count among the best in this genre that the craft-beer fan can try.

A little later John takes us through the brewery. Menno has excused himself because he has to catch a plane to Oslo for meetings.

WITH OUR BEERS WHAT WE'RE LOOKING FOR IS BALANCE AND HARMONY – NOT A BITTERNESS RECORD.

Apart from the two owners de Molen has ten employees. In 2014 they produced about 500,000 litres (130,000 gallons); in 2015 it had probably become 7000 (185,000). The growth is constant and self-funding. Earlier about 90 per cent of the volume produced was exported. But very slowly, word about the extraordinary quality is beginning to get around in their own country. Nevertheless about 75 per cent is still exported to more than 30 different countries.

Despite their great success since, Menno and John haven't forgotten their roots as brewers. Just as before, the people here see themselves as part of an experimental brewery. 'We're simply not satisfied when we don't also regularly brew something outside our normal program,' says John. At least every six weeks therefore they make a brew the like of which has never yet been seen in Bodegraven – and will also probably never be seen again.

The brew kettle and storage tanks sport *Star Wars* motifs: Luke Skywalker, Han Solo, Princess Leia. Both John and Menno are big fans. In the next building are the bottling plant, storage space and a warm room where the beers are matured with a final bottle fermentation. Among others are also those that before too long will be stored in wooden barrels. They must be carbonised before they are sold – after their time in the barrels they contain practically no more perceptible carbon dioxide.

What strikes us straight away on our tour is the pronounced casual and happy working atmosphere. Wherever we go, we see laughing, jokes and friendly, helpful people. A further sign of the very special spirit that reigns at de Molen is the up to ten disabled people who work on the first floor as part of an integrative project on hand-labelling and packing small special brews. Here too a visible pride and joy in their work reigns.

The Brouwerij de Molen doesn't offer classic sight-seeing tours. But it's still worth making a pit stop in Bodegraven – for example on the way to Amsterdam. In the windmill there's a restaurant with ten different de Molen beers on tap and more in bottles. The beer shop, also in the windmill offers, besides their own beers, an exquisite choice of products from allied breweries.

And also, for whoever would like to get to know the brewery completely from up close, there's still an opportunity once a year: de Molen is well known for its cooperation with many allied breweries. Since 2009 Menno and John have organised on their property the Borefts Beer Festival on the last weekend in September, at which a considerable proportion of the European craft-beer scene's crème de la crème have a family reunion.

nä

SOLO
MOUT & MOCCA
26-03-15
2480

bar

BROUWERIJ

WE DON'T HAVE COMPETITORS, WE HAVE COLLEAGUES.

Roast chicken with barbecue sauce

ROAST CHICKEN WITH BARBECUE SAUCE

Juicy soft chicken with a truly crispy crust in best Vienna style! And it comes with a spicy home-made barbecue sauce – YEE-HAA!

PREPARATION
45 minutes

METHOD

For the barbecue sauce: Peel the onions and cut into thin wedges. Heat the oil in a frying pan and fry the onions until golden brown. Finely dice the garlic and sun-dried tomatoes and add to the pan. Sprinkle in both paprikas. Stir in the tomato paste and brown sugar. Mix in 250 ml (8½ fl oz/1 cup) of water with the plum jam and the diced tomatoes, and bring to the boil. Add the beer and balsamic vinegar. Cook, uncovered, stirring frequently, for 25–30 minutes until thick. Season with salt.

For the roast chicken: Wash the chicken pieces under cold water. Mix with the lemon zest and juice, paprika and pepper. Coat in the flour, dredge through the egg and then roll in the breadcrumbs, pressing them on well. Leave on a baking tray lined with baking paper for 15 minutes for the crumbs to 'stick on'.

Heat some oil for deep-frying to 170°C (340°F) in a deep-fryer or a heavy-based high-sided saucepan (the oil is at the right temperature when bubbles rise from the handle of a wooden spoon held in the oil). Working carefully and in batches, fry the chicken pieces for 10 minutes, turning now and then. Drain on paper towel and season with salt. Serve with the barbecue sauce.

TIP: If you don't want to cut the chicken into pieces yourself, ask your butcher for two wings; two thighs; two drumsticks; and two boneless breasts, each halved.

BEER STYLES: The most varied beer styles suit this dish, from fresh dry pilsner through spritzy kölsch to darker and maltier styles.

SPECIAL RECOMMENDATION: The Pale Ale by Sierra Nevada, Chico, California, USA (see p. 221) – a true classic and nothing less than a milestone. Not too intense to dominate the chicken but with enough strength and personality to sustain the barbecue sauce.

INGREDIENTS
Serves 2–4

Barbecue sauce

- 200 g (7 oz) small onions
- 3 tablespoons oil
- 1 garlic clove
- 4 sun-dried tomatoes
- large pinch of smoked paprika
- 1 tablespoon sweet paprika
- 1 tablespoon tomato paste (concentrated purée)
- 100 g (3½ oz) soft brown sugar
- 50 g (1¾ oz) plum jam (jelly)
- 500 g (1 lb 2 oz) diced tomatoes
- 50 ml (1¾ fl oz) malt beer
- 2 tablespoons balsamic vinegar
- salt

Roast chicken

- 1 × 1.2 kg (2 lb 10 oz) chicken, cut into 10 pieces (see Tip)
- finely grated zest and juice of ½ organic lemon
- 1–2 teaspoons sweet paprika
- freshly ground black pepper
- 80 g (2¾ oz) plain (all-purpose) flour
- 2 medium eggs, lightly beaten
- 300 g (10½ oz) breadcrumbs
- salt
- oil, for deep-frying

LIME QUARK DROPS WITH FRIED GINGER PINEAPPLE AND CASHEW NUTS

INGREDIENTS
Serves 4

Quark drops
finely grated zest and juice of 1 organic lime
600 g (1 lb 5 oz) creamy quark
2–3 tablespoons sugar

Ginger pineapple
20 g (¾ oz) fresh ginger
8 pineapple slices
3 tablespoons sunflower oil
60 ml (2 fl oz/¼ cup) India pale ale
2 tablespoons pineapple jam (jelly)
45 g (1½ oz/¼ cup) roasted, salted cashew nuts, roughly chopped

Sweet and sour lime quark with ginger-hot fried pineapple slices, accompanied by salted cashew nuts – and hidden somewhere on the plate is another lemon-fresh IPA, which also tastes very good with this meal!

PREPARATION
20 minutes (plus at least 5 hours for the quark drops to hang)

METHOD
For the quark drops: Mix the lime zest and juice with the quark and sugar. Thoroughly wash out four clean tea towels (dish towels). Divide the quark between the towels, putting it in the middle of each one, then close the towels over the quark and tie up tightly with kitchen twine. Hang the packages up to drip, for example over the sink. Leave for at least 5 hours and preferably overnight.

For the ginger pineapple: Peel the ginger and grate finely. Heat the oil in a non-stick frying pan and sear the pineapple slices for 2–3 minutes on each side. Deglaze with the beer. When it boils, stir in the ginger with the pineapple jam. Boil quickly to thicken.

Carefully remove the quark drops from the towels and sit them on serving plates. Add the pineapple slices (hot or cold), scatter over the cashew nuts and serve.

TIP: Fresh pineapple tastes better than tinned.

BEER STYLES: IPA, pale ale, fruit lambic, gueuze.

SPECIAL RECOMMENDATION: 11/05 Session IPA – Citra by Brew By Numbers, Bermondsey, England, which is exclusively hopped with highly aromatic citra hops. The citrus aromas that give these hops their name meld with the ginger and pineapple to form a summer-fruit triad.

Lime quark drops with fried ginger pineapple and cashew nuts

APPLE MUFFINS WITH CARAMEL SAUCE

INGREDIENTS
Makes 12

Apple muffins
125 g (4½ oz) butter, plus extra for greasing
50 g (1¾ oz) caster (superfine) sugar
2 teaspoons vanilla sugar
salt
2 eggs
150 g (5½ oz/1 cup) plain (all-purpose) flour
1 teaspoon baking powder
1 tablespoon milk
1 apple (e.g. elstar, golden delicious)
50 g (1¾ oz) ground hazelnuts

Caramel sauce
100 g (3½ oz) sugar
200 ml (7 fl oz) pouring (single/light) cream
1–2 pinches of ground coffee

caramel popcorn, to serve (optional)

Airy, juicy apple muffins are thickly iced with warm caramel sauce. You couldn't wish for more.

PREPARATION
40 minutes (plus 20 minutes to cool)

METHOD
For the apple muffins: Preheat the oven to 200°C (400°F). Beat the butter, sugar, vanilla sugar and a pinch of salt with an electric mixer until foamy. Beat in the eggs one at a time. Mix the flour and baking powder then stir them into the egg mixture with the milk. Peel the apple, grate finely and stir into the dough with the hazelnuts.

Divide the dough between the holes of a muffin tin greased with butter. Bake on the lowest shelf for 20–25 minutes until golden brown. Remove from the oven and leave to cool in the tin.

For the caramel sauce: Bring the sugar, cream and coffee to the boil and cook, stirring constantly with a wooden spoon, until a light-brown caramel sauce forms (about 10 minutes).

To finish: It tastes best when the muffins are still lukewarm and are drowned in the caramel sauce. Serve scattered with the popcorn, if you like.

BEER STYLES: Strong, malt-flavoured beers like bock, doppelbock, barley wine or imperial stout.

SPECIAL RECOMMENDATION: KBS by Founders Brewing Company in Grand Rapids, Michigan, USA. One of the best barrel-aged imperial stouts worldwide. Brewed with a hint of coffee and vanilla makes it the perfect match for these muffins.

Apple muffins with caramel sauce

CHICO, USA

SIERRA NEVADA

SIERRA NEVADA

In a little more than 35 years the craft-beer old hand Sierra Nevada has blossomed from the smallest garage brewery to the seventh biggest brewery in the United States. The annual production comes to more than 150 million litres (40 million gallons). An American success story.

'In principle, we still do exactly the same thing we did when we were still brewing in 20 litre [5 gallon] bins,' says the founder of Sierra Nevada, Ken Grossman – and he's thoroughly conscious of the coyness of this statement. Because the time when he still brewed in 20 litre bins has long past. In building on a second site on the East Coast alone he has gone through around US$100 million – and the sales numbers have reached a level that even industrial giants would be happy with in Germany.

In the meantime, it's become difficult to continue viewing Sierra Nevada as a craft brewery. But they still brew in Chico, California, with the same passion and the same desire for extraordinary quality as on the first day. Just as before, people here see themselves as part of the craft movement, and a multitude of cooperative ventures with small young breweries demonstrate the close contact they still maintain with that scene.

The success story began in Chico with US$100,000 borrowed from within the family circle – because Grossman could not convince a bank that his business plan would work. After almost a decade of successfully gathering experience as a hobby brewer, in 1979 he founded his brewery of the same name on the edge of the Sierra Nevada. 'At that time there weren't that many possibilities for buying interesting beers. And so I simply decided to brew them myself,' Grossman says. On 15 November 1980 – after ten brews, none of which had satisfied Grossman's standards – the first Sierra Nevada pale ale appeared on the market. It was made with Cascade hops, which today are *the* hops of the craft-beer scene per se. At that time it was an obscure cultivar, originally raised to replace the disease-prone Mittelfrüh hops. Because of their hugely intense fruity aromas they were seen as unsuitable by the large American breweries. For the craft-beer pioneers it was, however, exactly these aromatics that made the new breed interesting.

Today, Sierra Nevada's flagship signature brew pale ale remains the same. In 1980 the first IPA followed. The two styles are the company's 'bread and butter' beers, responsible for the majority of the annual turnover. But in the last three decades

IN PRINCIPLE, WE STILL DO EXACTLY THE SAME THING WE DID WHEN WE WERE STILL BREWING IN 20 LITRE [5 GALLON] BINS.

things haven't stood still. A lot has changed: with the craft-beer boom, the head office in Chico has become a much-visited tourist attraction. The range of beers offered has widened enormously: apart from the ales they have Nooner, a remarkably quaffable, full-bodied pilsner; under the label Ovila Belgian-style abbey beers are produced in collaboration with an American Cistercian order; and many specialties brewed only seasonally round out the program. Most recently they proudly announced in Chico a collaboration with Brauhaus Riegele in Augsburg, Germany, to produce an authentic Oktoberfest beer. Even a kölsch appears in the extensive brewing portfolio.

Constant innovation is still an important theme for Sierra Nevada today. 'We haven't forgotten our roots. We experiment just as before, in order to brew the most amazing beers possible,' Grossman says. The best example for this attitude is Torpedo Extra IPA, which after the pale ale is probably the brewery's best-known beer, now even quite widely available in Germany, for example. It was the first IPA from Sierra Nevada available year round, and from its introduction in 2009 has been a great success. The impressive hop flavours of the beer rely on a technical innovation that also ultimately gave the beer its name: the hop torpedo. Instead of hopping in the typical IPA way by throwing the hops in the fermenting or storage tanks, in Chico only whole hop cones are used, no pellets, and are placed in a metal cylinder through which the maturing beer is pumped constantly. The result: an intense aroma yield with a simultaneously rather more moderate bitterness.

Another example is the Brux, a cooperation with the American craft-beer legend Russian River. To be able to produce this beer, which is bottle-fermented with 'wild' yeasts, with constant quality, they specifically installed a modified pharmaceutical dosing unit that injects with high precision a defined amount of the hard-to-handle yeasts directly into each bottle before it's closed. Yet another example of Californian innovativeness is the Hop Hunter beer – also widely available in Germany – which allows IPA fans to enjoy a beer with 'green' (i.e. undried) hops outside hop harvest season. In addition to normal hopping, it's hopped with an oil that's extracted immediately after the hop harvest in an especially gentle steam process. In this way, therefore, Hop Hunter has exactly the same intense citrus aromas and floral notes as only beers hopped with wet hops (fresh green hops) have otherwise.

It's not without pride that Ken Grossman looks back on what he has achieved in the past 30 years: 'When I founded the firm, American beer was considered a bad joke. Today brewers visit us from Germany to study how we brew our beer!' It seems as though the 59-year-old is still determined to continue his mission to provide the world with better beers.

SIERRA NEVADA BREWERY
PALE ALE
SIERRA
TORPEDO

Chocolate brownie cake with orange and braised figs

CHOCOLATE BROWNIE CAKE WITH ORANGE AND BRAISED FIGS

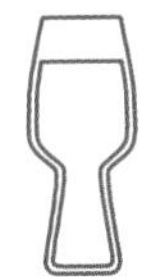

The classic brownie in a party version, with sweet chocolate, beer and orange marmalade. It's served with figs tossed in honey and beer, and a cool orange and sour cream sauce.

INGREDIENTS

Serves about 12

Cake

- 200 g (7 oz) dark couverture chocolate
- 200 g (7 oz) butter
- 3 medium eggs
- 100 g (3½ oz) caster (superfine) sugar
- 50 g (1¾ oz) sour cream
- 50 ml (1¾ fl oz) beer
- 100 g (3½/⅔ cup) plain (all-purpose) flour
- 1 level teaspoon baking powder
- 1 tablespoon unsweetened (Dutch) cocoa powder
- 50 g (1¾ oz) ground hazelnuts
- 150 g (5½ oz) orange marmalade

Figs and sauce

- finely grated zest and juice of ½ organic Valencia orange
- 100 g (3½ oz) sour cream
- 50 ml (1¾ fl oz) thickened (whipping) cream
- about 2½ tablespoons honey
- 8 figs
- 2 tablespoons oil
- splash of beer

PREPARATION

15 minutes (plus 30 minutes to bake and about 45 minutes to cool)

METHOD

For the cake: Preheat the oven to 180 °C (350 °F). Finely chop the chocolate. Melt the butter in a saucepan, then remove from the heat and stir in the chocolate until melted. Beat the eggs and sugar for 5 minutes until thick and creamy.

Mix the sour cream and beer together until smooth, then mix into the egg mixture. Stir in the chocolate mixture. Sift together the flour, baking powder and cocoa, then fold in with the ground hazelnuts. Line a 22 cm (8¾ in) springform tin with baking paper cut to fit. Pour the batter into the tin and bake for 30 minutes. Cool in the tin.

For the figs and sauce: To make the sauce, mix the orange zest and juice with the sour cream, cream and ½ tablespoon of the honey until smooth. Wash and halve the figs. Heat the oil in a frying pan then toss the figs with the remaining honey for 1–2 minutes. Season with a splash of the beer.

To finish: Melt the orange marmalade in a small saucepan. Remove the cake from the tin and brush the top with the marmalade. Cut the cake in half horizontally. Brush the bottom half with the remaining marmalade, then replace the top half. Serve with the figs and sauce.

BEER STYLES: Dark bock, porter, stout and imperial stout.

SPECIAL RECOMMENDATION: Organic Chocolate Stout by Samuel Smith, Tadcaster, England. The organic cocoa it's brewed with builds an aromatic bridge to the chocolate on the plate. More than just a pairing – it's a marriage!

BERLINER WEISSE JELLIES

INGREDIENTS
Serves 4–6

4 leaves gelatine
330 ml (11 fl oz) Berliner weisse
100 ml (3½ fl oz) woodruff syrup*
1 tablespoon sugar
100 g (3½ oz) sour cream
1 tablespoon vanilla sugar
juice of ½ lime
100 ml (3½ fl oz) thickened (whipping) cream

*

Woodruff syrup *is made from a sweetly aromatic plant and is available online or from specialty stores.*

This green jelly (jello) for grown-ups is a true food of the gods – cool, refreshing and sweet, but with stimulating sourness – and best gobbled up on a sun deck.

PREPARATION

15 minutes (plus at least 5 hours to cool)

METHOD

Soak the gelatine in cold water. Heat the Berliner weisse beer, woodruff syrup and sugar in a saucepan. Squeeze out the gelatine and dissolve it in the beer mixture. Pour into serving glasses.

Refrigerate the jellies for at least 5–6 hours to set. Mix together the sour cream, vanilla sugar and lime juice. Whip the cream to stiff peaks and fold into the sour cream mixture. Top the heavenly jelly with the cream and . . . enjoy!

BEER STYLES: Berliner weisse or gose.

SPECIAL RECOMMENDATION: Londonerweisse infused with gin botanicals by Beavertown Brewery, England, with herbal notes that harmonise beautifully with the woodruff. Or look for one of the awesome oak-aged Berliner Weisses of De Garde Brewing in Tillamook, Oregon, USA.

Berliner weisse jellies

SOUR BEER

KRIEK

The starting beer is always a lambic. Near the end, with fruits added it goes into a wooden barrel, where it ripens for six weeks. With traditionally made krieks a second fermenation occurs in the bottle. These krieks (called 'oude', or old) are bone-dry, but in modern versions the fermentation is stopped in favour of a slight residual sweetness.

ORIGIN	Belgium
CHARACTER	Sour and fresh, strongly fruity and bone-dry
FERMENTATION	Spontaneously fermented (with *Brettanomyces* etc.)
ALCOHOL CONTENT	3.5–8% Vol.
DRINKING TEMP	5–9°C (41–48°F)
BEST GLASS	Beer tulip; Balloon glass
EXAMPLES	Cantillon's Kriek, Boon Kriek's Mariage Parfait
RECIPES	Sweet Beer Waffles (see p. 231), Yoghurt Mousse (see p. 232)
VARIANTS	Framboise (raspberries), pêche (peach), lambics with rhubarb, currants or grapes. Closely related to other sour beers such as gose or weisse.

Sweet beer waffles with sour cherries and vanilla yoghurt

SWEET BEER WAFFLES WITH SOUR CHERRIES AND VANILLA YOGHURT

The krieks and fruit lambics go superbly with patisserie and as an accompaniment to cherry desserts. Here delicious Trappist beers give the sweet waffles a very special flavour.

PREPARATION
40 minutes

METHOD

For the sour cherries and vanilla yoghurt: Combine the sour cherries in a saucepan with the sugar and 50 ml (1¾ fl oz) of the beer, and bring to the boil. Mix 2 tablespoons of beer with the cornflour and stir into the boiling cherries. When the cherries begin to thicken, remove from the heat and transfer to a bowl. Allow to cool, stirring occasionally.

Mix the vanilla seeds with the yoghurt, cream and extra sugar, stirring until smooth. Add a little lemon juice.

For the waffles: Using an electric mixer, beat the butter with 30 g (1 oz) of the sugar and a pinch of salt until pale and fluffy. Separate the eggs. Beat the egg whites with a clean electric mixer (there must be no fat on the beaters!), then beat in the remaining sugar until shiny. Beat the egg yolks together then beat into the butter mixture.

Mix the flours and baking powder and gradually fold into the butter and yolk mixture with the beer, milk and egg white. Leave the batter to rest for 5 minutes. Heat a waffle iron to medium, grease it lightly with oil, then add 2 tablespoons of the batter and cook for 4–6 minutes until golden brown. Repeat with the remaining batter to make ten to twelve waffles. Sprinkle with pearl sugar before serving, if liked.

Serve the waffles with the sour cherries and vanilla yoghurt.

BEER STYLES: Fruit lambic, kriek

SPECIAL RECOMMENDATION: A beer trio from Belgium: intensely cherry-flavoured Lindemans Kriek for the cherries; a shot of the Trappist beer Chimay Rouge Première for the waffles; and as an accompaniment one of the best sour ales in the world, the kriek Mariage Parfait by Boon – highly complex flavour symphony based on sour cherries.

INGREDIENTS
Serves 4

Sour cherries and vanilla yoghurt
300 g (10½ oz) frozen sour cherries
1 tablespoon sugar, plus extra to taste
80 ml (2½ fl oz/⅓ cup) kriek beer
1–2 teaspoons cornflour (cornstarch)
1 vanilla bean, split lengthways and seeds scraped
100 g (3½ oz) yoghurt
50 ml (1¾ fl oz) pouring (single/light) cream
lemon juice, to taste

Waffles
125 g (4½ oz) softened butter
120 g (4½ oz) caster (superfine) sugar
salt
3 eggs
150 g (5½ oz/1 cup) plain (all-purpose) flour
100 g (3½ oz/¾ cup) buckwheat flour, or 100 g (3½ oz/⅔ cup) extra plain (all-purpose) flour
1 teaspoon baking powder
100 ml (3½ fl oz) strong beer
100 ml (3½ fl oz) milk
oil, for greasing
pearl (nib) sugar (optional), to garnish

YOGHURT MOUSSE WITH CARAMEL AND MERINGUE

This airy fresh mousse of yoghurt and cream is made entirely without gelatine and tastes so good you'll want to gobble it up. You needn't have it only with caramel sauce, toasted pine nuts and meringue, by the way – you should also try variations with fruit sauces and fresh fruit.

INGREDIENTS

Serves 4–6

500 g (1 lb 2 oz/2 cups) thick full-fat yoghurt
120 g (4½ oz) sugar
1 tablespoon lemon juice
400 ml (13½ fl oz) thickened (whipping) cream
1 teaspoon vanilla sugar
2 tablespoons pine nuts
6 small meringues, plain or coffee-flavoured
caramel sauce (see p. 218)

PREPARATION

20 minutes (plus time to hang)

METHOD

Wash a clean tea towel (dish towel) out with hot water, then use it to line a colander over a bowl. Mix the yoghurt with the sugar and lemon juice until smooth. Whip the cream with the vanilla sugar to stiff peaks and fold into the yoghurt. Transfer the mixture to the lined colander. Close the towel over the mixture and leave in the colander to drain overnight in a cool place.

The next day turn the mousse out onto a platter. Toast the pine nuts in a dry frying pan until golden brown, allow to cool then roughly chop. Finely crumble the meringues and scatter everything over the mousse. Just before serving, drizzle over some caramel sauce, and serve with the remaining caramel sauce on the side.

BEER STYLES: Bock, doppelbock, weizenbock, barley wine. If you're a fan of fruitiness, grab some kriek or fruit lambic.

SPECIAL RECOMMENDATION: One of the awesome beers of Wicked Weed Brewing, Asheville, North Carolina, USA. Choose a fruit-driven sour like the Angel of Darkness or a non-fruity option like the coffee/vanilla-dominated Silencio – both will accompany the mousse in a different, but equally delicious, way.

Yoghurt mousse with caramel and meringue

AROMATIC

WITBIER

Formerly an almost extinct Belgian variety of wheat beer. Based on barley malt and unmalted wheat. Traditionally flavoured with orange peel and coriander seeds. Yeast-clouded, straw-yellow and strikingly pale. Refreshingly fruity and aromatically deep. Drunk cold.

ORIGIN	Belgium
CHARACTER	Sour and fresh, aromatic
FERMENTATION	Top-fermented
ALCOHOL CONTENT	4–7% Vol.
DRINKING TEMP	6–8°C (43–46°F)
BEST GLASS	American-wheat-beer glass
EXAMPLES	Hoegaarden's Wit Blanche, Hitachino Nest White Ale, Blanche de Namur
RECIPES	Sausages in an Onion Broth (p. 158), Venison Schnitzel (p. 131), Stilton with Blood Orange (p. 204)
VARIANTS	none

Mango with marzipan crumbs and a vanilla yoghurt lime sauce

MANGO WITH MARZIPAN CRUMBS AND A VANILLA YOGHURT LIME SAUCE

Ripe sweet mango with marzipan crumbs hot from the oven, with a cool vanilla yoghurt and lime sauce – and a cold beer, the perfect accompaniment to sweet dishes.

PREPARATION

25 minutes

METHOD

Slice off the unpeeled mango cheeks on either side of the stone. Score the flesh in a lattice down to the skin on each mango half. Give the skin a gentle push in the middle to make a 'mango hedgehog'. Sit each half, skin side down, on a baking tray lined with baking paper. Preheat the oven to 220°C (430°F).

Mix the marzipan paste with the butter and breadcrumbs. Quickly rub in the butter with your fingers, until you have sweet crumbs. Scatter the crumbs over the mangoes. Bake for 6–8 minutes until the crumbs are golden brown.

Meanwhile, cut the remaining mango flesh from the stones, removing the skin. Purée in a food processor with the vanilla yoghurt, sour cream, lime zest and juice, and vanilla sugar. Serve the sauce with the baked mangoes.

BEER STYLES: A perfect dish for the exotic fruity flavours of many IPAs. Alternatively, pale ale or wheat beers go well.

SPECIAL RECOMMENDATION: Tropical Torpedo by Sierra Nevada, Chico, California (see p. 221). A cornucopia full of tropical fruits in the glass meet mango, lime and vanilla on the plate. A drop dead gorgeous match!

INGREDIENTS

Serves 4

- 2 ripe mangoes
- 100 g (3½ oz) raw marzipan paste
- 50 g (1¾ oz) cold butter, diced
- 100 g (3½ oz/1 cup) dry breadcrumbs
- 100 g (3½ oz) vanilla yoghurt
- 50 g (1¾ oz) sour cream
- finely grated zest and juice of ½ organic lime
- 1–2 teaspoons vanilla sugar

DOUGHNUT SOUFFLÉS WITH RASPBERRY SAUCE

INGREDIENTS

Serves 6

Soufflés

softened butter, for greasing
3 tablespoons breadcrumbs
3 jam (jelly) doughnuts
2 medium eggs
pinch of salt
50 ml (1¾ fl oz) thickened (whipping) cream

Raspberry sauce

300 g (10½ oz) frozen raspberries, thawed
juice of ½ lemon
100 g (3½ oz) raspberry jam (jelly)
125 g (4½ oz/1 cup) fresh raspberries
icing (confectioner's) sugar, to taste

They're called Berliners in Germany, where they're especially loved on Shrove Tuesday and at New Year, but wherever you are, deep-fried jam (jelly) yeast doughnuts, are bound to be a favourite. As an airy soufflé, however, they should find a place on dessert plates all year round.

PREPARATION

20 minutes (plus 20 minutes to bake)

METHOD

For the soufflés: Lightly grease a 6-hole muffin tin with butter and coat with the breadcrumbs. Preheat the oven to 200°C (400°F).

Halve the doughnuts crossways and scrape out the filling. Finely dice the doughnuts – this is easiest using a bread or other serrated knife. Separate one of the eggs, then whisk the white with the salt until stiff using an electric mixer. Whisk the egg yolk and the whole egg with the cream. Mix in the doughnut pieces, then fold in the beaten egg white. Spoon the mixture into the prepared muffin tin. Bake for 20 minutes.

For the raspberry sauce: Purée the thawed raspberries with the lemon juice and jam, then pass this sauce through a sieve. Drizzle the sauce onto serving plates, and divide the fresh raspberries between them. Remove the soufflés from the oven and set each one in the middle of a plate. Sift over the icing sugar. Serve immediately.

TIPS: A scoop of vanilla ice cream makes this fun!

Instead of raspberry sauce, strawberry sauce, vanilla sauce, vanilla yoghurt or chocolate sauce are great.

BEER STYLES: Berliner weisse or Belgian gueuze. For raspberry fans, Belgian framboise.

SPECIAL RECOMMENDATION: Any framboise will do – but if you happen to get hold of it, take the one from Cantillon, Brussels, Belgium (see p. 119). Their Rosé de Gambrinus is the blueprint of a fruit lambic brewed the classic way: uncompromisingly fruity and unashamedly sour. Which in this case is not that much of a problem – as the soufflés are sweet enough.

Doughnut soufflés with raspberry sauce

KRIEKBIER
Liefmans
Hornbeer
närke
närke
KULTURBRYGGERI
CARNIOLA
IMP
Tonjaks!
AMARO
black damnation
Lief & Leed
la Goudale
L'UNA
L'UNA
HOP HEAD
NOËL
EXTRA
ReAle
Guld
CROCE di MALTO
Platinum
GINGER
BEER
Pilsener

AN APOLOGY . . .

. . . AND A FEW BOOKS

So many beers. So many breweries. So little room: Many other breweries and beers earned a portrait within the frame of this book. Schlenkerla in Franconia, for example, or Andreas Gänstaller in Schnaid near Bamberg. Or one of the Trappist Breweries in Belgium, above all the one Westvleteren, with the 'best beer in the world'. Or a representative of the diverse Italian beer scene, such as Teo Musso of Birra Baladin. And in the craft-beer world there are also lively Scandinavians, with brewing legends like Mikkeller. We apologise to everyone who also deserves to be named. Perhaps it will work out in the end with a second volume of Cooking with Craft Beer!

For everyone who can't wait that long and already wants to deepen their knowledge of the craft-beer world, we've put together a few recommendations for further reading:

Barley & Hops: The Craft Beer Book by Sylvia Kopp, Gestalten, 2014
This detailed work by the beer sommelier and founder of the Berlin Beer Academy gives a further overview of the subject.

Cocktalian: Bier & Craft Beer by *Mixology* magazine, Tre Torri, 2014 (German)
A just as detailed (right up to homebrewing recipes!) beautifully presented compendium of the craft-beer universe. The explanations of food pairing come from our own recipe writer, Stevan Paul.

Beer Styles from Around the World by Horst Dornbusch, Master Brewers Association of the Americas, 2015
Portraits of 117 different beer styles, with accompanying recipes in quantities for professional (100 litres/ 26 gallons) and homebrewers (20 litres/5 gallons).

Craft-Bier selber brauen: die Revolution der Heimbrauer by Fritz and Heike Wülfing, Lempertz, 2014 (German)
A small but powerful tour through the world of craft beers and homebrewing. Written by one of the doyens of the scene (see p. 147).

The Brewmaster's Table by Garrett Oliver, HarperCollins, 2005
The standard work on food pairing from the master brewer of New York's Brooklyn Brewery.

The Oxford Companion to Beer by Garrett Oliver, Oxford University Press, 2011
The English-language reference work on beer from the same author.

INDEX

INFORMATION ABOUT BEER

PROFILES

BEER STYLES

RECIPES

A

B

C

D

E

F

H

ACKNOWLEDGEMENTS

This book would not have been possible without a damn lot of support. First of all, of course, the breweries whose profiles appear in this book, who opened their doors to us and took time out for us and let us try their magnificent beers. For the trust that entails, we're very, very thankful.

ALE-MANIA
www.ale-mania.de

BOGK BIER
twitter.com/bogkbier

BRLO
www.brlo.de

CANTILLON
www.cantillon.be

DE MOLEN
www.brouwerijdemolen.nl

FERAL BREWING
www.feralbrewing.com.au

HOFSTETTEN
www.hofstetten.at

KERNEL
www.thekernelbrewery.com

KEHRWIEDER KREATIVBRAUEREI
www.kreativbrauerei.de

SCHNEIDER WEISSE
www.schneider-weisse.de

SCHÖNRAMER
www.brauerei-schoenram.de

UERIGE
www.uerige.de

VORMANN
www.vormann-brauerei.de

But brewing and storage tanks don't shine with extremely interesting knowledge and also don't offer helpful comments or other support. For that you need people. Like, for example:

2Cabecas
Beerbods
Rita Bihler
Andreas Bogk
Brauerei Neuzelle
John Brus
Melissa Cafferata
Bernardo Couto
Andy Dickerson
The DO Lectures
Hans-Peter Drexler
Flying Turtle Beer
Peter Frühwirth
Andreas Gänstaller
Ken Grossman
Matt Guyer
Johannes Heidenpeter
Hopfenland Hallertau Tourismus e.V.
Will Irving
Maira Kimura
Sylvia Kopp
Sabine and Peter Krammer
Christian Kraus
Hannah Kupsch
Katharina Kurz
Christian Laase
Michael Lembke
Daniel Lichter
Markthalle Neun
Martina Mayer
Bernd Müller
Dirk Myny
Menno Olivier
Pax Bräu
Stephanie Poltinger
Peter Read
Anja Reinhardt
Evin O'Riordain
Elisabeth Rose
Sebastian Sauer
Georg Schneider VI
Christoph Tenge
Teresa's Café
Eric Toft
Tourism Australia
Tanja and Oli Trific
Ulrich Karl Tröger
Julie, Magalie, Jean and Jean-Pierre van Roy
Brendan Varis
Richard Voit
Felix vom Endt
Pauline and Christian Vormann
Ute Wachendorf
WBB Willner Brauerei Pankow
Julia and Oliver Wesseloh
Heike and Fritz Wülfing

Without them all, this book would not have become the gem it now is.

CHEERS!

CONTRIBUTORS

STEVAN PAUL, *Recipes & food styling*

Born in 1969, lives in Hamburg. This trained chef works as a recipe developer, food stylist and cookbook author for book and magazine publishers. He also writes culinary articles and columns for magazines and newspapers. Since 2008 he has written his blog at nutriculinary.com, one of the most-read food blogs in the German-speaking world.

WWW.STEVANPAUL.DE

TORSTEN GOFFIN, *Author*

Lives and works in Cologne. After several years as a photographer in the advertising industry, he moved from the world of images to the world of words. He now works as a TV writer, gastro-journalist and tertiary educator, writing primarily for the long-running German TV show *SoKo*. Since 2009 he has written 'Allem an Anfang', his blog on 'eating, drinking and other forms of culture'.

ALLEMANFANG.TUMBLR.COM

DANIELA HAUG, *Photographer*

Daniela Haug was a freelance producer on international film projects, until co-founding as:if Film Matters in London. In 2001 she moved to Berlin, where she produces films and web projects for such customers as Mercedes Benz, West German Radio and many others. Her photography is published in the areas of food, travel, art and cars, and in 2014, in the bestselling *Auf die Hand*, with Stevan Paul.

WWW.DANIELAHAUG.COM

MIRIAM STROBACH, *Graphic design*

Born in 1982 in Bavaria, she grew up in Hesse and Carinthia (Austria), and now lives in Vienna. She studied communication design in Graz and developed her love of cuisine in Paris. As a co-founder of Le Foodink, she conceives and creates projects in the field of food and drink.

WWW.LEFOODINK.COM

TANJA TRIFIC, *Styling*

Tanja Trific has worked in Hamburg for many years as a stylist for print media and the advertising industry. In 1990 she began as a stylist and producer for *Schöner Wohnen* magazine, and since 2001 has worked as a freelance stylist in the lifestyle and food areas.

This edition published in 2017 by Smith Street Books
Melbourne | Australia | smithstreetbooks.com

First published in German as *Craft Beer Kochbuch*
by Christian Brandstätter Verlag in 2015

ISBN: 978-1-925418-48-4

CIP data is available from the National Library of Australia

TRANSLATOR: Nicola Young
TEXT: Torsten Goffin
RECIPES & FOOD STYLING: Stevan Paul
PHOTOGRAPHY: Daniela Haug
STYLING: Tanja Trific
ART DIRECTION & DESIGN: Miriam Strobach, Le Foodink
DESIGN ASSISTANCE: Martina Kogler, Le Foodink
PROPS: www.diy-stock.de, thanks to Maren Somfleth; www.das7tezimmer.de, thanks to Gabriele Kos

Picture credits:
Hopfenland Hallertau Tourism (Anton Mirwald) pp. 10, 128;
Sierra Nevada pp. 220–23

Printed & bound in China by C&C Offset Printing Co., Ltd.

Book 36
10 9 8 7 6 5 4 3 2 1